E

M000118923

Series

Strong and Courageous
The Character and Calling of
Mature Manhood

Derek Brown

GBF Press
Sunnyvale, CA

Strong and Courageous
The Character and Calling of Mature Manhood

Strong and Courageous: The Character and Calling of Mature Manhood
Copyright © 2017 Derek Brown

Published by GBF Press.

For more titles, please visit our website at GBFPress.com.

Requests for information about GBF PRESS can be sent to:

GBFPress@gbfsv.org

All rights reserved.

ISBN-13:978-0692892084
ISBN-10:0692892087

Scripture quotations are from the ESV® Bible (The Holy Bible,
English Standard Version®), copyright © 2001 by Crossway, a
publishing ministry of Good News Publishers. Used by
permission. All rights reserved.

Cover Design: Bob Douglas

This work is a publication of GBF Press. No part of this
publication may be reproduced, stored in a retrieval system, or
transmitted in any form or by any means except by permission of
the publisher.

Dedicated to the men of
Grace Bible Fellowship
Sunnyvale, California

Contents

Acknowledgements

This book was a challenge and a joy to write. It was a challenge because I was convicted by the biblical call to mature manhood as I wrote. It was a joy because I was encouraged by Christ in those same Scriptures to pursue godly manhood with renewed intentionality. But this book was also a joy to write because I had the opportunity to work with several excellent proofreaders and editors as I entered the final stages of this project. Special thanks to Bryan Lee, Nikki Lee, Jasmine Patton, Landon Liles, Michael Enos, Breanna McManis, and Cliff McManis for your keen editorial comments and corrections. Thank you also to Jasmine Patton for preparing the Scripture index. Thank you to Bob Douglas for the excellent cover design. Thank you to P. J. Tibayan, Rick Zaman, and Justin Peters for reading through the manuscript and offering some very gracious endorsements. Finally, I want to thank my wife Amy who consistently encourages me in my pursuit of godly manhood. Books may have one author, but they are always a team effort. Thank you to everyone who helped make this book better.

Introduction

In the introduction to his book, *Men to Boys: The Making of Modern Immaturity*, Gary Cross, professor of history at Penn State, makes a stinging observation about young men in America.

> Everywhere I turn today I see men who refuse to grow up—husbands of thirty-five who enjoy playing the same video games that obsess twelve-year olds; boyfriends who will not commit to marriage or family; and fathers who fight with umpires or coaches at their son's little league games. We all know of men in their thirties or forties who would rather tinker with their cars than interact with their families, fathers who want to share in their children's fads, and even bosses and political leaders who act like impulsive teenagers. Many are frustrated and confused about what maturity is and whether they can or want to achieve it. I call them boy-men. A common query (really a complaint) today, especially from women, is, where have all the men gone? What they seem to imply is that perfectly normal men who in previous generations would have been expected to be grown-ups continue to act, look, and think like teenagers.[1]

Do any of these observations resonate with you? Perhaps you recognize that you personify a few, if not many, of Cross's pointed indictments. Perhaps you notice these traits characterize some of the young men in your life—sons, nephews, sons-in-law, grandchildren—and you are concerned about their future and their impact for Christ.

Cross continues in the rest of his book to give sociological and historical reasons for why men of the so-called millennial generation (those born between 1982-1992) tend to remain in perpetual immaturity. And yes, there are important sociological and historical reasons why guys in my generation just can't seem to grow up. But what Cross is unable to do, despite his erudition in the areas of sociology and history, is get to the root of the problem.

What is the basic problem that afflicts not only my generation but *every* generation of men? It is that ever since the Fall, men have been afflicted with a tendency towards *passivity*. What is passivity? Passivity is a *disposition to refuse or neglect to exercise God-given leadership in the face of clear and present responsibilities*. Instead of facing and making difficult decisions, reconciling broken relationships, protecting the vulnerable, confessing our sin, taking the blame for wrongs we've committed, providing financially for ourselves and for our families, disciplining our lives for the sake of godliness, fighting sin, serving those in need, and taking initiative to exercise godly leadership in our families, churches, school, and places of employment, we have a propensity to hide in a corner. The *primary* problem for today's men and our relationships is passivity.

But I'll even take it a step further. In the first chapter of this book we are going all the way back to the beginning of creation. We'll see that it was male passivity that led to

Adam's sin and brought about the entire Fall of mankind. Let that last sentence hit you. As we'll learn in our survey of Genesis 2 and 3, all the death and misery and sin that has come crashing into our existence was the result of *one man's passivity*. We will look specifically at where Adam failed, why he failed, and what resulted from his failure. But we will also see what God intends and has always intended for men, and then, I pray, find grace in Christ to be the courageous men that God wants us to be for His glory and the good of others.

In the remaining chapters of the book, I will develop a biblical vision of manhood, framing our discussion around the character (chapter 2) and calling (chapters 3, 4, 5) of mature manhood. We are to be men of courage and love (that's character), and those who lead, protect, and provide for others (that's the calling). In chapter six I broach a vital yet often neglected topic in our reflections on biblical masculinity: leaving father and mother. In this chapter I will argue that in order for us to become the men whom God has called us to be, we must leave father and mother. As we will see, this departure from our family of origin entails much more than geographical re-location.

In chapter seven I consider mature manhood specifically from the perspective of singleness. Much of the recent conversation on biblical manhood considers manhood with reference to marriage. This approach is entirely legitimate, for the Bible frames much of its discussion of manhood in the context of marriage. Nevertheless, marriage may not be the privilege of all Christian men, nor does marriage come to all men at the same age or stage of life. In other words, *all* men must cultivate their manhood in the context of singleness for at least some portion of their lives. Although I weave application to single men throughout the entire book, I consider specifically the various ways that single men can grow in godly masculinity in chapter seven.

In chapter eight I draw our conversation to a close by directing us to the resources that we will need in order to truly make strides in godly masculinity. The good news is that God has provided us with all the resources we need in the gospel, the Church, and the Holy Spirit. In our pursuit of godly masculinity, we have everything we need to become the men God has created and re-created us to be.

First, however, we need to go all the way back to the beginning of time in order to gain some insight into our plight as men. Making headway in our trek to mature manhood is inherently difficult because we will be traveling with a deep wound that, although treated and well on its way to being healed, still slows our pace and dogs our steps. In chapter one we are going to take a close look at our father, Adam, and make several observations of where, and, just as importantly, why he fell short in his calling as a man. From this investigation we will be able to draw some important conclusions about the nature of true manhood that will help us navigate the remaining portions of this book. We now turn to chapter one to consider the fallout from "one man's passivity."

1

One Man's Passivity: Twelve Observations on Male Leadership from Genesis 2-3

In this chapter I am going to make twelve observations from Genesis 2 and 3 with respect to male leadership. I will spend more time on some observations than others, but it's vital to examine each of these aspects of the Genesis narrative in order to lay a solid foundation on which to build the rest of this book. If we are going to understand what God intends for and requires of men, we need to go back to Genesis to see what happened in the Garden of Eden among Adam, Eve, God, and the crafty serpent. In order to get the most of this chapter, I encourage you to take a few minutes to read Genesis 1-3. By refreshing yourself with the Genesis creation narrative—or acquainting yourself for the first time—you will be better able to follow the flow of my argument and the next several observations.

Observation #1: God Creates Man First
With regard to our discussion of manhood, the first observation I want to highlight in the Genesis narrative is the fact that Adam is created first (see Gen 2:7). Upon an initial

reading of the biblical text, we might not consider this a noteworthy observation—the order of creation is simply a matter of fact, not a matter of significance. But as we will see in subsequent observations, this order signals something important about the man and woman's relationship generally and God's intention for man specifically. But beyond the immediate context, we also have inspired New Testament commentary that highlights the meaning of this order of creation.

For example, in the first letter to his young protégé, Timothy, the apostle Paul grounds his instruction regarding local church leadership in the order of Adam and Eve's creation.

> I do not permit a woman to teach or to exercise authority over a man; rather, she is to remain quiet. For Adam was formed first, then Eve; and Adam was not deceived, but the woman was deceived and became a transgressor (1 Tim 2:12-14).

In this passage, Paul limits church leadership—the office of elder, specifically—to men only. This prohibition has nothing to do with the man and woman's respective competence or intelligence. Paul is well aware of the Old Testament texts that exalt women and highlight their unique strengths and skills (e.g., Prov 31:10-31). Rather, Paul roots his instruction in chronology—in the fact that the man was created *before* the woman: "For Adam was formed first, then Eve."

Paul sees a clear signal emanating from the Genesis narrative in the detail that Adam was created prior to Eve. By bringing Adam into existence before his wife, God is telling us that Adam is to fulfill the role of leader (and, as we will see in this chapter and in the rest of the book, protector and provider). For the woman to exercise authority *over* the man is unfitting for the very reason that man was created first. Again, this is not a matter of superiority: both the man and the woman are made in the image of God.[1] Nevertheless, with regard to roles, God intends man to serve as the leader in his relationship with the woman. And the melody that God sounds here will resonate through the entire Old Testament into the New Testament: man bears the unique responsibility to lead.

Observation #2: God Entrusts Man with the Care and Guardianship of the Garden

Secondly, we see that the man is given the task of working and keeping the garden: "The LORD God took the man and put him in the garden of Eden to work it and keep it" (Gen 2:15). The word for "work" in this text refers to tilling the ground. Adam was instructed to work productively in the garden.

It is important to note here that work comes *before* the Fall. We will come back to this important truth in later chapters. For now it is enough to observe that God gave Adam work prior to the Fall and the subsequent curse of the ground (see Gen 3:17-19). Difficulty and futility in one's work would result after the Fall and curse, but work itself was given as a gift as a way that man would reflect his creative God and exercise dominion over the earth (see Gen 1:28-31).

So, men, if we are going to fulfill our manhood—if we are going to be the men that God created us to be at a very basic level—we must work. When we refuse to work and provide we are actually rebelling against a fundamental aspect of our personhood, as we will see in more detail later. God has created us to work, and we often suffer depression, lack of direction, and a sense of purposelessness when we refuse to engage in productive labor.[2]

What, specifically, was Adam called to do? He's called to cultivate the land. Using a little sanctified imagination, we might say that he would probably collect the fruit to eat, survey the land and see how it can be improved, and build useful tools and structures. He was to work the garden. But he was also called to *keep* it.

The word translated "keep" (ESV) refers to protection. Adam is to guard the garden from intruders. Interestingly, the presence of this responsibility assumes that there were intruders from whom the garden was to be guarded. Moses' language here is deliberate, and we will see the need for Adam's role a little later when we examine Genesis 3:1.

Observation #3: God Entrusts Man with the Divine Commandment

Thirdly, God gives Adam a command regarding what he is allowed to eat: "The LORD God commanded the man, saying, 'You may surely eat of every tree of the garden, but of the tree of the knowledge of good and evil you shall not eat, for in the day that you eat of it you shall surely die'" (Gen 2:16-17). Adam is given free access to every tree in the garden, but one. God's command here is not restrictive: Adam could choose from the myriad of trees in the garden and take of their fruit. As Sinclair Ferguson comments, "The use of the verb [commanded] is surely significant in this context: the enjoyment of plenty is the first element in the command; the prohibition of one tree is the second."[3] He was required to refrain from one tree—the tree of the knowledge of good and evil—but he had an abundance of other trees in which to delight. What is implied here and what is borne out in the rest of the narrative is that Adam would have been expected not only to obey this command, but also to teach it to anyone else who would be brought into the garden.

You might wonder how we know that Adam was intended to teach God's Word to whomever else would enter the garden. I believe we can gain some insight into this situation by asking these questions: Why did God give Adam the instruction prior to Eve's existence? Why not keep him from the forbidden tree until Eve's creation and instruct them both? I believe God is conveying something important with respect to how the man is meant to lead: Adam was to take responsibility to teach his family the Word of God and guard his family from false doctrine. Adam would have been expected to guard the garden from the infiltration of false teaching and anyone who would suggest that God's Word was not worthy to be obeyed.

These observations do not suggest that the wife has no part to play in this teaching and protection—indeed, Adam would have given her the instruction to guard the garden—but only that Adam, because he is the man, would have borne a unique responsibility to teach and protect his family from false teaching.

Observation #4: God Creates Eve from Adam's Body

After Adam was entrusted with the divine instruction on how to live in the garden, God brought to Adam all the animals He had previously created.[4] Adam names the animals, but we learn quickly that there was more to this exercise than ascribing proper names to these living creatures. Moses comments: "The man gave names to all livestock and to the birds of the heaven and to every beast of the field. But for Adam there was not found a helper fit for him" (Gen 2:20). God had a task for Adam to complete: for the sake of future

9

work in the garden and communication among other image-bearers, the animals needed names. But God also intended something else by assigning Adam this task of naming the animals. Adam needed a companion to help him work and keep the garden, and he needed to be certain that such a companion could not be found among the creatures already in existence. God would need to do something special to provide the man with his helper.

How did God solve Adam's dilemma? "So the LORD God caused a deep sleep to fall upon the man, and while he slept took one of his ribs and closed up its place with flesh. And the rib that the LORD God had taken from the man he made into a woman and brought her to the man." (Gen 2:21-22). From Adam's own body God formed his perfect complement, a woman. Adam responds with delight: "This at last is bone of my bones and flesh of my flesh; she shall be called Woman, because she was taken out of Man" (Gen 2:23).

Adam's joy was grounded in two profound realities. First, the woman was *like him* because she was created in God's image. Unlike the animals, the woman shared the man's nature: in her womanhood she reflected her Creator who had given her the responsibility to exercise dominion over the earth. But Adam's joy was also rooted in the reality that the woman was *not like him*. She was a *woman* and not a *man*: "She shall be called *ishah* (woman) because she was taken from *ish* (man)" (Gen 2:23). Adam rejoiced because he beheld in Eve both sameness and difference. She was an image-bearer, but she was also a woman. The woman's origin from the man communicates complementarity, and she is the perfect fit for Adam in every way: physically, emotionally, and spiritually. But there's more.

In his first letter to the Corinthians, the apostle Paul reflects on the Genesis account and identifies another vital theological truth in the description of how the woman came into existence. The fact that she was taken from the man is of particular importance.

> For a man ought not to cover his head, since he is the image and glory of God, but woman is the glory of man. For man was not made from woman, but woman from man. Neither was man created for woman, but woman for man (1 Cor 11:7-9).

In this passage, Paul is dealing with an issue at the church in Corinth related to the wearing of "head-coverings." While it is difficult to say exactly what these head-coverings were, the deeper theological reason for Paul's concern is clear. The wearing of head-coverings was a matter of reflecting one's masculinity or femininity, specifically with regard to one's role in marriage. The basic argument that Paul is making in 1 Corinthians 11:1-16 is that when the church is gathered, it is unfitting for a husband to adorn himself in a way that implies that he is in submission to his wife, or for a wife to adorn herself in a way that implies that she is not in submission to her husband. The deeper issue in this text is one of roles generally and leadership specifically, and Paul derives the basis for his argument in the fact that Eve was *taken from* Adam.

In other words, by creating the woman from the man, God was again signaling a distinction in roles, especially in relation to how Adam would be called to exercise leadership in this new relationship. When Paul says that, "Neither was man created for woman, but woman for man" (1 Cor 11:9), he is not endorsing a master-slave relationship. The woman was not created for the man in the sense that she exists merely to do the man's bidding. Rather, Paul is telling us that the Genesis narrative establishes man's role as leader, and we know this because the woman was created for the man, not vice-versa.

Men, we have lingered over these past few observations in order to deepen your conviction that your role as leader is grounded in the created order, and flows directly out of the biblical text. The impulse you feel to lead in your home, in the church, and in the public-square, and that sickening sense of failure when you yield to passivity and forsake your calling to lead, are not the artificial emotional constraints of a patriarchal society; they are the spiritual responses of those who have been designed by God and redeemed by Christ to fulfill a specific role.

Yes, there is such a thing as male domination and the abuse of leadership, but these are perversions of God's original design, not the exercise of it. Indeed, Paul himself is quick to add that in the Lord, the man is never independent of the woman, "for as woman was made for man, so man is now born of woman" (1 Cor 11:12). Nevertheless, it is the man upon whom God has placed the burden of leadership as we will see in our next observation.

Observation #5: The Man is to Leave
Father and Mother and Cleave to His Wife

We will examine this observation in more detail in chapter six, but it is important now to lay some of the groundwork for what I will say in later chapters and to establish the implications of this observation for godly male leadership. Note Genesis 2:24-25: "Therefore a man shall leave his father and his mother and hold fast to his wife, and they shall become one flesh. And the man and his wife were both naked and were not ashamed."

Have you ever read that passage and asked yourself, "Why does Moses say that only the man is to leave his father and mother? Isn't the woman supposed to leave her father and mother and cleave to her husband?" We know that it isn't Moses' intention to remove the woman's responsibility to leave her father and mother and cleave to her husband because the text itself says that the man *and* woman are to become one flesh. If they are to become one flesh, then it must be that she has to leave father and mother.

The reason why Moses is phrasing his commentary this way should be clear by now. The man must be the one who leads his wife out from their respective families of origin to create their own new family. If he doesn't fulfill this responsibility, it won't happen. Sure, the couple may live in a different house and join in sexual union, but if the man does not truly leave his father and mother, then he will not be able to lead his wife to leave hers, and the three families will become entangled in a way that will harm all the relationships involved and hinder the new couple's obedience to God.

Observation #6: The Serpent Bypasses the Man and Goes to the Woman

Not only do we have explicit statements in the Genesis narrative that highlight the man's responsibility to lead, we also find implicit evidence in the way Moses describes Satan's interaction with Eve. In other words, by the way Moses unfolds the story of Adam and Eve's temptation, he is teaching us something about male leadership.

Because God declared everything "very good" after he made the man and the woman at the end of day six, I am inclined to believe that Satan had not yet fallen into sin until after God made Eve. Nevertheless, regardless of where you place Satan's fall (whether it was before, during, or after the creation of man and woman), we know that he would have had opportunity to observe God create the man and set him in charge of the garden. He would have also seen the man's creation prior to the woman's, and the distinction between their respective origins (Adam from the dust of the ground, the woman from the man's side). Therefore, Satan would have had knowledge of the man and woman's differentiated roles prior to his act of deception.[5]

In light of this it is instructive to note that Satan bypasses the man in order to go straight to the woman with his question. By going to the woman first, Satan undermines the man's role of leadership and protection by placing the burden of spiritual defense upon the woman.

At this point we begin to observe that Adam is being tempted to yield to passivity, a character quality that will inevitably lead to sinful disobedience. Although God had tasked him with guarding the garden (Gen 2:15), the man merely stands by while a serpent slithers up to his wife and begins to question the Word of God. We know that Adam was there because the text tells us that the woman gave the fruit to her husband who was "with her" (Gen 3:6).[6] Yet, the man allows the enemy in the door undeterred.

There is an important lesson here, brothers. Satan chose one of God's creatures as his vehicle of deception. It's likely, because he often disguises himself as an angel of light (see 2 Cor 11:14), that Satan possessed an animal in order to fool the man and woman into believing that he was harmless. We need to be aware of this same strategy today. Satan will use God's good creatures to undermine your wife's obedience to and faith in God's Word. It may not be an animal, but it could be a friend, a book, a family member, or a TV show that subtly but surely weakens your wife's faith in, love for, and obedience to God's Word. As we will see, the vehicle is irrelevant. No matter who or what it is, once it begins to undermine God's Word, then man must shun all passivity and protect his wife from the wiles of the enemy.

Observation #7: The Serpent Questions and Misquotes God's Word, but the Man Does Nothing

When Satan approached the woman, his strategy was to question and misquote God's Word. Instead of meeting the serpent's subtle twisting of God's Word with prompt and decisive rebuke, the man just stood by watching.

What was happening?

> *Was he tempted to make excuses?* "I'm tired. The serpent is scary. I'm too busy handling my other responsibilities in the garden."

> *Was he tempted to relinquish his role as leader and protector?* "I'll just let her handle it."

> *Was he tempted by cowardice?* "If I say something I might cause a scene. I might offend my wife by stepping in to protect her."

Ultimately, we don't know exactly what was happening in the man's heart and mind. What we know is that the man simply observed the situation instead of correcting, teaching, and rebuking the serpent for the sake of his wife. Adam might have said, "Let's be very clear. We know exactly what God has said. Don't you dare come in here with your sophisticated questioning of God's Word. We won't have it in this family.

Leave." Such a response to the serpent's craftiness would have been difficult, but it would have most likely been effective. Adam may have had to stand his ground and endure several volleys from the enemy, but we know that when confronted with the truth of God's Word, Satan typically flees after multiple unsuccessful attacks (see Luke 4:1-13; James 4:7).

The tendency to become derailed by cowardice or distracted by our smart phones, YouTube, Netflix, or our various hobbies in the face of encroaching evil is deadly, and it afflicts all men to one degree or another. The world fell into ruin because Adam's unwillingness to confront false teaching led to his direct disobedience of God's Word, and our families and churches will fall into ruin if we stand by while our wives, children, and brothers and sisters in Christ are accosted by sincere-sounding angels of light. God calls Christian men to put away distractions and act courageously against false teaching for the sake of those whom He's entrusted to them.

Observation #8: The Serpent Contradicts God's Word, but the Man Does Nothing

It gets worse. Not only did Adam not act when he noticed the serpent questioning God's Word; he allowed the situation to continue unchallenged, even as the intruder deepened his hostility toward God's Word. "You will not surely die," the serpent stated emphatically (Gen 3:4) in response to Eve's repetition of God's commandment. After creating an atmosphere of doubt by asking misleading questions about God's Word, Satan now unleashes a direct assault on the commandment. Questioning leads to contradicting as the serpent opposes the clear words of God: "[B]ut the tree of the knowledge of good and evil you shall not eat, for in the day that you eat of it *you shall surely die*" (Gen 2:17, emphasis added).

Satan's strategy was obviously progressive in nature. He sought first to create an atmosphere of doubt that would negatively affect how Adam and Eve related to the Word of God. Once doubt was introduced through the question, "Did God really say?" Satan was now in a place to undermine Scripture more directly without opposition. And this is also how Satan will work in our families and in our churches. He will come at you first with a sincere-sounding question. We might be tempted to respond, "Oh, you're so insightful with that question! You sound very intelligent with your speculative inquiry into the truthfulness of God's Word!" Then, because Satan has disarmed us and robbed us of the resources by which to recognize bald-faced lies, he will usually follow this kind of questioning with a direct denial of clear statements in God's Word. That is what occurred in the garden that fateful day: the serpent spoke a lie to the woman without resistance because he had already disabled Adam from acting courageously and decisively.

Why? Well, by this point the contradiction doesn't sound too bad. Even if Adam did recognize the contradiction, he had to risk the humiliation of stepping in at this point and saying, "You know, I was watching a cat video on my iPhone and I messed up, but now this is going to end, serpent. You're done. It's time for you to leave!" Sadly, Adam is stymied into indecision because he may have learned that it is very difficult to make up for our passivity once we've arrived at a certain point. It's too embarrassing to go to our wives or children, admit that we were wrong, and reclaim the helm of leadership.

In Christ, however, we are granted the freedom from the tyranny of keeping up with what people think of us. Because we have died in Christ to the pursuit of our own glory, we do not need to strategize to protect our reputation among those whom we serve as leaders. We can confess our sins, mistakes, and lapses in judgment to those we are called to lead and protect, and reclaim the ground we lost as a result of our passivity. As we live in light of the gospel, we can find forgiveness from God (1 John 1:9) and from one another (Eph 4:32) when we sin. This forgiveness keeps us from wallowing in defeat and enables us to get back on course if we've strayed. Yes, we failed, and we must own our failure. But we will fall into another of Satan's traps if we allow our failure to keep us from reclaiming our responsibilities.

Observation #9: Satan Impugns God's Character but Adam Does Nothing

Following his direct contradiction of God's Word and the implication that God is a liar, Satan now further impugns God's character by suggesting to Eve that God is a stingy, envious Lord who likes to keep good things from His children. "For God knows that when you eat of it your eyes will be opened, and you will be like God, knowing good and evil" (Gen 3:5). You can almost hear the heretical hissing: "It's obvious why God threatened death to those who eat of the fruit of the tree. He wanted to keep you from ever attaining to His status in knowledge. He's keeping something good from you, and you should be suspicious of this kind of God."

But just as before, Adam was tempted to look upon his wife and the serpent with either indifference or fear, or a mixture of both. Whatever the case, he never stepped in with *truth* to combat the seduction of his wife by the crafty serpent. Yet, Adam had plenty of solid reasons to refute Satan's cunning strategy at this point. The idea that God was stingy and envious was laughable, especially in light of the fact that He had just created a world of unimaginable abundance and beauty, provided Adam with access to every tree in the garden except one, and formed for him a companion of perfect complementary fit. Indeed, as we already noted above, God's first command to Adam was to enjoy the abundance he had created. But instead of laughing and rebuking, the man stood by and allowed Satan to suggest to his wife that their good and gracious God wasn't nearly as good and gracious as He had revealed himself to be.

Observation #10: The Woman Listens to the Lie and Disobeys God, but the Man Does Nothing

Satan's strategy worked. He isolated the woman, undermined the leadership of the man, attacked the Word of God, and caused the woman to doubt God's goodness and disobey His clear command.[7] "So when the woman saw that the tree was good for food, and that it was a delight to the eyes, and that the tree was to be desired to make one wise, she took of its fruit and ate" (Gen 3:6). Again, Adam might have intervened at this point, but he does nothing as his wife is led away from the safety of faith and obedience into the peril of unbelief and disobedience.

Observation #11: The Woman Instructs the Man to Sin, and He Does

And so we are lead to eleventh observation in the latter part of verse six. The woman instructs Adam to sin, and he does. "So when the woman saw that the tree was good for food, and that it was a delight to the eyes, and that the tree was to be desired to make one wise, she took of its fruit and ate, and she also gave some to her husband who was with her, and he ate." (Gen 3:6). The key phrase in this verse is comprised of two little words, "with her." Up to this point Adam had been with his wife. While Satan questioned and contradicted God's Word and seduced his wife into danger, Adam stood by, unwilling to take care of business. Now the entire structure of the relationship has been turned on its head. Instead of lovingly teaching and *leading* his wife into faith and obedience for her joy and protection, he is *following* his wife into disobedience.[8] Previously, he did nothing. Now, he does something, and it's entirely the wrong move.

This is exactly how passivity works, brothers. We stand idly by while we should be leading, protecting, and providing for those entrusted to our care, and in response to our neglect our wives take the reigns of leadership. For a while we are happy to follow because now we won't have to work hard or make difficult decisions or exercise any courage. But beware! When we find ourselves enjoying the comfort of our wives taking the initiative to lead, protect, and provide for the home, we have greatly compromised our manhood, and trouble is only a few slithers away.

But lest we overcorrect our tendency toward passivity and steer into ungodly male domination, we must note that this text does not teach that men should refuse to listen to their wives. I've heard this verse used in such a way by men who apparently believe unilateral decision-making is an essential mark of strong leadership. But God does not rebuke Adam for merely listening to his wife (see Gen 3:17). If this were so, then a man would be in sin every time he received any kind of counsel from his wife. Rather, God rebuked Adam for listening to his wife *unto disobedience*. Included in the rebuke to Adam for listening to his wife was a reprimand for allowing the relationship structure between he and his wife to be reversed. When Adam should have been leading and teaching for the sake of righteousness, he was following and listening on the way to unrighteousness.

As we will discuss in more detail later in this book, one of the marks of a good leader is his willingness to listen to advice (see Prov 12:15). A strong leader is someone who is secure enough in Christ to take the good ideas from those around him, including his wife, and utilize them for the joy and fruitfulness of his whole family.

But in Adam's case, he didn't lead his wife into faith and obedience. And just when you think it can't get any worse, it does. Rather than leading his wife in repentance now that they have sinned, Adam attempts self-atonement by making clothing to cover their shame. "Then the eyes of both were opened, and they knew that they were naked. And they sewed fig leaves together and made themselves loincloths" (Gen 3:7).

As men, our temptation is to handle sinful situations like Adam did in the garden. Once we've allowed sin to occur in the family, either by actively committing it or passively allowing it, we will be tempted to cover that sin by lying, passing the blame (as we will see in the next observation), exchanging religious activity (church going, service, Bible study, etc.) for genuine repentance, or simply ignoring the problem. Mature Christian masculinity, however, will be quick to arrest his family's slide into self-atonement and either confess and repent of his own sin, or help his family members confess and repent of theirs.

Observation #12: God Goes to the Man First

In my judgment, this feature in the narrative powerfully

establishes the argument I've been making from the beginning of the chapter. Because God had entrusted the man with a unique role of leadership, He confronts the man first, despite the fact that it was Eve who ate of the fruit before her husband.

> And they heard the sound of the LORD God walking the garden in the cool of the day, and the man and his wife hid themselves from the presence of the LORD God among the trees of the garden. But the LORD God called to the man and said to him, 'Where are you' (Gen 3:8-9).

It is noteworthy that although Eve was the one who initiated the disobedience by first eating of the fruit and then persuading her husband to eat, it was Adam who receives God's initial rebuke. We might expect God to conduct the confrontation in reverse: go to the one who committed the first sin and led others to participate in their rebellion. This order of rebuke would have made sense *if* the man had not been entrusted with the unique calling to lead his family in obedience to God's Word. But by going to Adam first, God not only reaffirms the man's role as leader, He also implicitly rebukes Adam for his passivity. When a husband allows those under his protection and leadership to sin, he is held accountable for his failure; to bear this weight of responsibility before God is the burden Christian masculinity. Yes, Eve would be punished for her own part in the rebellion, but Adam bears a unique liability for their collective sin, because God had made him the head of his family.

Therefore, when there is unchecked sin in our children, or a breech in our relationships with our wives or our sisters in Christ, it is our responsibility, brothers, to remedy the situation, even if the children or the women in our life are primarily to blame. For example, if for some reason an obvious emotional distance has developed between you and your wife, there is nothing stopping her from initiating reconciliation, and wives are welcome to seek out biblical reconciliation with their husbands. But if this becomes the pattern—even when she is to blame—we are in danger of compromising our masculinity. Mature Christian manhood is characterized by swiftness in initiating reconciliation, even when the fault was not primarily ours (see also Matt 5:23-26). The supreme example for initiating reconciliation is seen in Christ. The fault was entirely ours, yet Christ *came to us* to initiate and complete the reconciliation.

Sadly, in the case of Adam, he not only failed to remedy the rift between him and his wife, he blamed his wife for the mess in which they found themselves. But again, this is exactly how passivity works. First, we are happy to let our wives take the lead because it means we can relax and remove the yoke of leadership from our shoulders. But once something goes wrong, we are quick to blame others—especially our wives—rather than facing the problem of our own passivity and taking the blame for not leading well.

One Man's Passivity

So here we have the fall of the entire human race into ruin, and it's no exaggeration to say that all the death and sin and ruin and filth and destruction and tragedy in this world is the result of *one man's passivity*. And men, it is no exaggeration to say that our passivity will wreck everything—in our homes, with our families, and in our church.

But lest we despair under the weight of conviction, there is one more feature in the narrative we must see. Again, it's important to note the order of the story. Adam and Eve have sinned, and their punishment for sin is coming: Eve and her female progeny will suffer pain in childbirth; man's livelihood will be afflicted by thorns and thistles. But *before* God levels his curse against his disobedient children, he *promises a redeemer.*

> The LORD God said to the serpent, "Because you have done this, cursed are you above all livestock and above all beasts of the field; on your belly you shall go, and dust you shall eat all the days of your life. I will put enmity between you and the woman, and between your offspring and her offspring; he shall bruise your head, and you shall bruise his heel" (Gen 3:14-15)

This is the first promise in the Bible of a man—the offspring of the woman—who will come to set everything right. The promised Redeemer will crush the one who tempted Adam and Eve to sin. What is significant is that the promise comes immediately *after* the confrontation with Adam and Eve but *prior* to the curse. God promises restoration before He levels the bad news of future struggle and suffering.

Men, this should give us great hope. While there are temporal consequences for our passivity—consequences we may be experiencing right now—we must keep in mind that our God is a God of redemption and restoration. By the very nature of our design as men, we are, as Douglas Wilson aptly notes, in a position of *"inescapable leadership."*[9] Manhood is serious business. But Jesus Christ is in the business of taking cowardly, indecisive, self-centered, passive boys and turning them into courageous, forward-thinking, self-sacrificing, leadership-initiating men. Through the power of the gospel we can become the men God has created and recreated us to be. And with that note of hope, let's turn to the following chapter and reflect on the character of mature manhood.

2

The Character of Mature Manhood: Courage and Love

From 2014-2016 the state of California endured a period of record drought. Some have said it was the worst drought in one hundred years. The lack of adequate rainfall devastated agriculture, decimated farms, impeded employment, and impacted the economy at local, state, and national levels. And despite recent rains, California remains, by and large, a parched land.

Though devastating, there's a drought among us that is even more troubling than California's lack of water. And the effects of this drought have crept into the church and are beginning to devastate individual churches and families. It's a drought of manhood. In subtle and not so subtle ways, men in our society are being discouraged from exercising leadership. We are hearing messages from cultural pundits that suggest it is arrogant and oppressive for men to take the helm of leadership in the home, the church, and various work settings. There is even resistance to the idea of male chivalry and the notion that men should serve women in culturally appropriate ways.[1]

Satan has done a great work to confuse men and instill in

them a suspicion that the desire to lead is a symptom of pride or a mere cultural hangover from a patriarchal era. For the sake of the church and the world, we need to talk about the character of mature manhood.

Courageous Intentionality

There is a danger, however, in talking so much about manhood. I've succumbed to this danger in my own life, and I've seen good friends encounter and yield to this danger at some point in their struggle over what it means to pursue godly manhood. The more we talk about the various contours of biblical manhood, the more we will find that passivity lies at the very center of our problems as men.

And it's true: most of our troubles as men are due to our reluctance to embrace our God-given calling to lead. We saw this truth illustrated vividly in the last chapter. So, the danger doesn't lie in the discovery that passivity is a deep and pervasive problem that will tempt us to forsake our calling as men. That's actually a helpful insight. The danger lies in our *response* to this insight.

See, if you're at all like me—and I suspect you are, even if we don't have much else in common—you will hear this call to reject passivity and look immediately to activity as the solution. But the answer to passivity is not mere activity, but *courageous intentionality*.

The first step on the road to godly masculinity is to cultivate true courage. Adam, as we saw in the last chapter, crumbled in the face of an immediate threat. When he should have been fearlessly protecting his wife from the wiles of the crafty serpent, he stood by, watching. And much of the biblical storyline from the garden onward consists of one of two scenarios: triumph as the result of masculine courage or tragedy in the absence of it.

Ever since that fateful day in the garden, men have been faced with spiritual and physical enemies, difficult decisions, challenging circumstances, and the possibility of loss. Whereas courage enables a man to obey the Lord when confronted with these harsh realities of life, cowardice entices a man to take the path of least resistance for the sake of self-preservation. If we are going to fulfill God's calling on our lives as men, brothers, the cultivation of courage must be of utmost concern.

Act Like Men

We see this call to masculine courage in 1 Corinthians 16:13 when Paul instructs the Corinthians: "Be watchful, stand firm in the faith, act like men, be strong." Paul's vital admonition comes at the end of his first letter to the Corinthian church. This church had serious problems among its members, including rampant, unchecked sexual immorality, the misuse of spiritual gifts, selfishness, and a host of other serious issues that Paul addressed throughout his letter. But in his final comments, Paul offers several straightforward exhortations: "Be watchful, stand firm in the faith, act like men, be strong."

Act like men? That seems like an odd way to address the Corinthian church. Weren't there any women in this congregation? Yes, there were, and Paul had written directly to the women several times in this letter (see 1 Cor 7:4, 8, 10-16, 34, 39-40; 11:3-15; 14:34-35). So why end his letter with this kind of statement? Because Paul is drawing on a truth that we've already seen in the first three chapters of the Bible that is reaffirmed through the rest of the Old Testament: as the men go, so go the people of God. If Corinth is going to make any progress out of the morass that they're in, their success will be dependent, in large measure, on the men acting like men. The same goes for your family and your church.

The word translated "act like men" in the ESV and NASB is the Greek word ἀνδρίζεσθε (*andrizesthe*). This word is often used in the Septuagint (the Greek translation of the Old Testament) and translated as "be strong and courageous" or simply "be courageous" (e.g., Josh 10:25; 2 Sam 13:28; 2 Chron 32:7). Universally in the Old Testament this word is used in reference to men, and it's often used when people are being led out to battle.

With this background from the Septuagint, I take Paul's use of the word in the context of his letter to a local congregation to indicate that the apostle is placing the responsibility to lead upon the *men* in Corinth. But not only is Paul placing the responsibility to lead upon the men, he is also using this particular word to signal that courage is at the heart of godly manhood. Courage is essential if these men are going to lead the Corinthian church out of the doctrinal and practical troubles in which they find themselves. Courage will be necessary if the men at Corinth are going to "be watchful" and "stand firm in the faith." Courage is needed because our roles and our responsibilities as men will require us to make hard decisions, to take risks, and to lead others in true doctrine and practical godliness.

But the development of courage is not the result of marshaling our will power and grinding out obedience when confronted with trying circumstances. Such an approach to courage will often lead to one of two extremes: irremediable discouragement in the face of failure, or harsh, overbearing, sporadic attempts at leadership. Neither of these is the fruit of genuine courage, for courage does not flow from the strength of our own wills, but from faith in God's promises. We see this connection between faith and courage illustrated in the book of Hebrews.

In Hebrews 11:1-40, we are given several examples of Old Testament saints who accomplished great things for God because they were empowered and emboldened by believing in God's promises of future blessing and a spiritual inheritance. In several cases, courage was required to act in obedience to God's call. In each of these instances, it was faith that provided the needed courage.

> By faith Abraham obeyed when he was called to go out to a place that he was to receive as an inheritance. And he went out, not knowing where he was going. By faith he went to live in the land of promise, as in a foreign land, living in tents with Isaac and Jacob, heirs with him of the same promise. For he was looking forward to the city that has foundations, whose designer and builder is God. . . . By faith Moses, when he was grown up, refused to be called the son of Pharaoh's daughter, choosing rather to be mistreated with the people of God than to enjoy the fleeting pleasures of sin. He considered the reproach of Christ greater wealth than the treasures of Egypt, for he was looking to the reward (Heb 11:8-10, 24-26).

Notice that it was *faith* in a future reward that enabled Abraham and Moses to act in courageous obedience. If we are faced with temporal loss and difficulty, the only way we can give up what is valuable to us—possessions, comfort, reputation—is if we are certain that we will someday receive an inheritance that makes the troubles of this life pale in comparison to the glory we will experience (see also 2 Cor 4:17-18). When it comes to godly masculinity, it is faith, and faith alone, that unlocks the courage we need to carry out God's call to lead in the home, the church, our place of employment, and in the public square.

But courage must be guided in the right direction, so godly masculinity requires *intentionality*. We might heed the call to resist passivity and cultivate courage, but we will find ourselves soon discouraged and confused if we are not channeling our activity and boldness in a specific direction.

Scripture extols the virtue of intentionality in both the Old and New Testaments. Proverbs, for example, praises diligence, planning, thoughtfulness, and the pursuit of wisdom (Prov 4:7, 26; 12:24, 27; 20:18; 21:5). In the New Testament, we find Jesus exercising unwavering intentionality. He had divinely-mandated priorities to which He held, even when outside expectations didn't match these priorities (see Luke 4:43; 9:51).

Paul expressed his intentionality often. "I make it my ambition," Paul tells the Roman church, "to preach the gospel, not where Christ has already been named, lest I build on someone else's foundation" (Rom 15:20). Whether at home or in the body, Paul's aim was to please Christ (2 Cor 5:9). The goal of his teaching was love from a "pure heart and a good conscience and a sincere faith" (1 Tim 1:5). He confessed to the Corinthians that he did not run his Christian race aimlessly (1 Cor 9:26), and he instructed the Thessalonians to "aspire to live quietly, and to mind your own affairs, and to work with your own hands, as we instructed you" (1 Thess 4:11). To the Ephesians Paul said, "Look carefully then how you walk, not as unwise but as wise, making the best use of the time, because the days are evil. Therefore do not be foolish, but understand what the will of the Lord is" (Eph 5:15-17). Over and over Scripture exhorts men not only to pursue courage, but to adorn and direct that courage with intentionality.

What does courageous intentionality look like? We will learn in the following chapters the specific areas in which men are called by God to exercise their masculinity which will help us understand better what it looks like to be intentional. What is important to capture now is that the exercise of godly leadership will be thoughtful, well-planned, grounded in biblical priorities, and mostly proactive rather than reactive.

Practically, men, this means we will need to *spend time* thinking over every area of responsibility with which we've been entrusted for the sake of making sound decisions and noting areas for improvement. You may not think of yourself as a self-reflective person and confess that such habits do not come naturally to you. Organization and long-term planning are a struggle for you and always have been. Nevertheless, intentionality in your leadership will require you to spend regular time reflecting on how you are stewarding your leadership.

Leadership Characterized by Love

But there is one more element to godly masculinity that we must include before we move on. Immediately after Paul instructs the men in Corinth to be watchful, strong, and courageous, he gives a piece of instruction that is meant to motivate and flavor the godly man's every activity. "Let all that you do be done in love" (1 Cor 16:14). Just as there is the danger of jumping right into mere activity as the answer to passivity, so there is also the danger of mistaking male dominance for godly leadership. If our efforts to resist passivity and develop a heart of courage are not motivated by a love for those we are leading, then what is intended to be beneficial will turn beastly, and what is meant for good will lead to harm. We may say a lot of good things, but it will just be noise to our hearers (see 1 Cor 13:1-3).

I cannot emphasize this point enough. Leadership is *not* a right to claim for the glory of our own reputations.[2] Leadership is a burden we bear for the good of others. If we do not do all things in love as Paul instructs, we run the risk of dominating rather than leading those under our care. We also run the risk of mistaking unilateral decision-making for genuine leadership.

Therefore, *everything* that we do as men must be done in love. It's no coincidence that Paul would put love and courage together in 1 Corinthians 16:13-14. Paul knows himself, and he knows what happens to guys when they're told to "act like men!" The temptation is to respond to this exhortation with unreflective, thoughtless zeal. But love tempers all our actions with kindness, gentleness, patience, forgiveness, and a willingness to forbear the weaknesses of those we lead (see 1 Cor 13:4-8; see also 1 Thess 2:7-8).

What is Love?

When I refer to the primacy of love in Scripture generally and in the area of mature manhood specifically, I am not referring merely to warm feelings we might have toward others. Rather, I am talking about genuine affection for the people under our care that expresses itself in concrete acts of service and life-giving leadership. While heart-felt affection is an essential quality of love (see 1 Peter 1:22), Scripture never detaches this affection from the truth. That is why Paul said, when describing the character of authentic love in his first letter to the Corinthians, "love does not rejoice in wrong doing, but rejoices in the truth" (1 Cor 13:6). True love, therefore, is biblically-informed love.

But how do we define love? The simplest way to define love is to say that *love seeks what is best for the other person.* We can find this definition in Jesus' own statement in John 15:13: "Greater love has no one than this, that someone lay down his life for his friends." Jesus' death on the cross secured our deliverance from the wrath of God and provided us with peace with God, wholly apart from our works or inherent righteousness (see Rom 3:21-26; 4:5). Jesus' love for us compelled Him to do what was best for us: rescue us from eternal wrath and bring us into fellowship with God. In the same way, Christ's disciples are to "love one another," by laying down their lives for the good of others.

But in order to *do* what is truly good for others, we must first *know* what is good for others. That is why Paul prays that our love would grow "with knowledge and all discernment" (Phil 1:9). Our spiritual senses must be continually honed by the Word of God so that we might recognize the will of God and truly labor for the good of others (see Rom 12:1-2; Eph 5:17). We might have affection for those we lead, but unless we are informed by Scripture as to what is most beneficial to them, we will not lead them in what is best.

For example, if you believe that what is best for your child is an Ivy League education, academic and athletic achievement, wide and varied life experiences, and a lucrative post-college career, then your love for them will guide you to make these attainments the priorities in his or her life. But is teaching our children to focus on these kinds achievements what is *best* for them? While success in each of these categories can be a blessing and may serve to make us more useful in God's kingdom, none of these are the priorities of Christ's disciples. What is most important—what is best—for those we lead is that they come to know and walk in faithfulness to Jesus Christ (see 1 John 2:3-6). It might be that faithfulness to Jesus leads us to pursue an education at Harvard or Yale. And faithfulness to Jesus will always require us to perform our work with excellence (Eph 6:5-9). But love for those whom we lead will dictate that we make their character our paramount concern, not the location of their college or the number of letters after their name.

Love Provides Wisdom

Love is essential to the task of leadership because love enables us to act with wisdom. This is because true, Spirit-endowed love enables us to perceive people, events, and situations from a proper perspective and to make decisions accordingly. Bitterness and resentment blur our vision; love gives us clarity. As one author has rightly noted, "It is love which sees straight, thinks clearly, and makes us balanced in our outlook, judgments and conduct."[3] Even the great Reformer John Calvin observed that love empowers the Christian to act with wisdom. "To sum up," Calvin wrote centuries ago, "love will give every man the best counsel."[4] When one's heart is full of love, they do not need a long list of rules or situation-specific principles in order to make God-honoring decisions that benefit others. As we are informed by Scripture and walk by the Spirit, God Himself teaches us how to love those we lead (see 1 Thess 4:9).

Practically, love enables us to deal with others tactfully. J. Oswald Sanders defines tact as "intuitive perception, especially a quick and fine perception of what is fit and proper and right."[5] Loving leadership is not unreasonable or forceful, but sensitive to the needs of people in a given set of circumstances. Sanders continues, "[Tact] alludes to ones ability to conduct delicate negotiations and personal matters in a way that recognizes mutual rights, and yet leads to a harmonious situation."[6] Paul says it this way: "Love…is not arrogant or rude. It does not insist on its own way; it is not irritable or resentful" (1 Cor 13:4-5). James says it like this: "But the wisdom from above is first pure, then peaceable, gentle, open to reason, full of mercy and good fruits, impartial and sincere. And a harvest of righteousness is sown in peace by those who make peace" (James 3:17-18). Love provides us the wisdom with which we can navigate difficult situations with sensitivity and care.

Love Empowers Courage

As it turns out, it is love that actually enables us to act in courage. Paul makes this connection explicit in his first letter to Timothy when he reminds the young pastor that "God gave us not a spirit of fear, but of power and love and self-control" (2 Tim 1:7). We can understand the contrast between fear and power, but fear and love? What's the connection? Paul juxtaposes fear and love because he knows that genuine affection for people enables us to labor for their benefit, even when confronted with difficulties. "Love is the only power greater than fear," as one author has wisely observed. "When one truly loves God and his neighbor enough to give himself for them, fear is cast out."[7]

Paul also knows that Spirit-empowered courage is not an obnoxious brashness or recklessness. Courage—if it is going to endure and be useful to others—must be fueled by love. We will often find that cowardice likes to wear the guise of impudence and forcefulness. This leads to inconsistent jolts of pushiness, not true leadership. Love, however, enables us to move gently yet steadily and decisively ahead with our plans to labor for the good of others.

As we proceed into these next few chapters, we will discover that courage and intentionality are essential to the cultivation of mature manhood. But without love, all our efforts will come to nothing (see 1 Cor 13:1-3). Keep this vital point in mind as you read the following pages. Reflect much on God's love to you (Rom 5:8) and ask Him to stir your heart to love those under your care.

We now turn to our discussion of leadership.

3

The Calling of Mature Manhood: Leadership

In the next three chapters, I want to focus on three essential qualities of mature manhood. We saw in the previous chapter that courage, intentionality, and love are the foundation on which we can build the next three aspects of true leadership. We will now discuss the following characteristics of mature manhood.[1]

> Out of a heart of courageous love, mature manhood senses and assumes a God-given responsibility to **lead**, protect, and provide for those under his care, for their temporal and eternal benefit.

I've chosen these words very carefully. I say that mature manhood "senses and assumes" the responsibility to lead, protect, and provide because there may be times when a man is unable to fully assume one or more of these responsibilities. For example, it could be the case that a man has been injured either in his mind or his body and is therefore unable to work and to provide financially for his family. But just because he is unable to *assume* the responsibility, does not mean that the mature man does not *sense* the calling to do so. Although he may be unable to provide for his family at this particular time, the mature man would love to do it. He desires to provide for his family and for those around him, but due to his physical condition, he is unable to for this particular season.

The Blessing of Godly Male Leadership
As we noted briefly in the last chapter, the idea of male leadership seems to be under significant attack in our society. Sadly, the rejection of male leadership is the rejection of God's blessing because God intends that good leaders be a source of prosperity for His people. We see this in the life of David. Note David's words from 2 Samuel 23:3-4:

> The God of Israel has spoken; the Rock of Israel has said to me: When one rules justly over men, ruling in the fear of God, he dawns on them like the morning light, like the sun shining forth on a cloudless morning, like rain that makes grass to sprout from the earth.

Despite his sin, the kingdom had flourished under David's wise, humble, God-centered leadership. David's rule was characterized by justice and in the fear of God, and as a result, Israel enjoyed spiritual and material prosperity. Godly male leadership was like warm sun and pleasant, life-giving rain. We do well to keep this truth at the center of our thinking about male leadership. Men are tasked with leadership to *bless* those under their care and to labor for their good.

Godly Male Leadership Takes the Initiative

But how do men lead others for their blessing? In order to truly lead, a man must *take the initiative*. And he must not take the initiative only once or twice, but continually throughout his life. Why? Because leadership, by definition, is antithetical to the passivity we saw in chapter one. Adam, among other things, *waited* for someone else to fulfill his responsibility to guard his wife from the serpent. Because he didn't take the initiative at a crucial moment, we are today experiencing the tragic fallout from his failure to step out in bold leadership. But in what ways are men expected to take the initiative? We will look at six specific areas.

To Set the Example

First, men are called to take the initiative to set the example. A man deficient in character, integrity, or a personal walk with Jesus Christ is not able to lead effectively in any area of his life. We must be able to say to those under our care and within our sphere of influence, "Be imitators of me as I am of Christ" (see 1 Cor 11:1). This does not suggest that we must be perfect or sinless before we can start leading. Perfection is impossible in this life and we will always be troubled by some measure of sin and weakness on this side of heaven.[2] Nevertheless, genuine leadership demands that we make progress in personal holiness and spiritual growth so that we demonstrate authenticity in our leadership. We cannot lead others spiritually to a place where we have not already been, nor will we win the confidence of those under our care if we preach but do not practice (see Matt 23:3).

To Cast a Biblical Vision

Second, men are called to lead by casting a biblical vision for those under their care and within their sphere of influence.

One might think that this notion of casting a vision derives mainly from contemporary leadership theory rather than Scripture. But the responsibility to cast a vision is not the exclusive prerogative of corporate CEOs. Casting a vision is vital because it enables obedience to God's Word and motivates our followers to continue following us. "A real leader's aim," one author observes, "is to make everyone around him better. He makes them stronger, more effective, and more motivated."[3] People are strengthened, made more effective, and motivated when they are captured by a biblical vision. That is why we find regular examples throughout the Scripture of men casting a vision for their people.

We find Moses casting vision as he tells Israel to follow him into the wilderness. He reminds them of God's goodness and tells them of future reward so they are able to hope in God through their troubles (see Deut 8:1-9:5). We see Samuel encouraging Israel to repent of their sin of asking for a king on the basis of God's goodness and kindness (see 1 Sam 12:20-23). We see the prophets reminding disobedient Israel of God's intention for his people and His plan to restore them in the future (Jeremiah 29:11-13; 33:11; Zeph 2:7).

But best of all we see Jesus casting vision as He gathered His disciples for ministry. In a brief, concise sentence, Jesus shows us how to cast vision for those whom God has entrusted to our care.

> From that time Jesus began to preach, saying, "Repent, for the kingdom of heaven is at hand." While walking by the Sea of Galilee, he saw two brothers, Simon (who is called Peter) and Andrew his brother, casting a net into the sea, for they were fishermen. And he said to them, "Follow me,

and I will make you fishers of men." Immediately they left their nets and followed him (Matt 4:17-20).

Notice how Jesus calls His disciples. He first says, "Follow me." He could have stopped here if He chose to. Jesus was the self-authenticating God-man, and His very presence and the words "Follow me" could have induced obedience on their own. But Jesus does more than just call for immediate obedience. He provides these men with compelling motivation. "Follow Me, *and I will make you fishers of men.*" Follow Me, and you will be part of something bigger than yourself. Follow Me, and I will transform you into the men you were created to be. Follow Me, and you will experience the joy of living for the eternal benefit of other people. *That's* vision, and it creates happy followers.

Men, there are plenty of opportunities to cast vision in your respective spheres of influence. In your local church, for example, you can cast vision in order to draw a few other men around you to begin a weekly prayer and Bible study meeting. Explain to your brothers why regular fellowship, prayer, and corporate reflection on the Scripture are vital disciplines in their walk with Christ. If you've been entrusted with a ministry at your church, take the initiative to cast a compelling biblical vision for the servants in that ministry.

Husbands, take some time to craft a vision for your family. Write down spiritual goals, hopes, and dreams for your family, and set that document in a place where you will be regularly reminded toward what you, your wife, and children should be striving. If you've been invested with leadership responsibility at work, think of ways to develop a culture of integrity, respect, and diligence among your colleagues. If you are a single man in a dating relationship, take the initiative to cast a vision for your girlfriend about how you desire the relationship to proceed, how you plan to protect her emotional and physical purity, and what you believe a godly romantic relationship entails.

To Plan for the Good of Others

Third, men must take the initiative in planning for the good of others. After we take the initiative to establish a biblical vision for those within our sphere of influence, we must apply that vision with concrete strategies for implementation. Again, we are drawn to the example of Jesus as he proactively planned for the good of His disciples during the Passover immediately preceding his death on the cross.

But before we study this particular example of Jesus planning for the good of His disciples, we must step back into a time before history to grasp the theological foundations for this idea. Specifically, we must consider what God the Father and God the Son were doing before the very foundation of the world.

Prior to creation, God the Father was making specific, detailed, well-ordered plans with his Son for the good of His people. Note carefully the language of *planning* in Ephesians 1:3-10:

> Blessed be the God and Father of our Lord Jesus Christ, who has blessed us in Christ with every spiritual blessing in the heavenly places, even as he *chose us in him* before the foundation of the world, that we should be holy and blameless before him. In love *he predestined us* for adoption to himself as sons through Jesus Christ, *according to the purpose of his will*, to the praise of his glorious grace, with

which he has blessed us in the Beloved. In him we have redemption through his blood, the forgiveness of our trespasses, according to the riches of his grace, which he lavished upon us, *in all wisdom and insight* making known to us the mystery of his will, *according to his purpose*, which *he set forth* in Christ *as a plan* for the fullness of time, to unite all things in him, things in heaven and things on earth (emphasis added).

Before the foundation of the world, God the Father was making plans with His Son to save His people. The method, the means, and the final goal of salvation were all charted before God said, "Let there be light" (Gen 1:3). And when the Son came into the world, He continued in this pattern of planning for the good of His people.

On the feast of Unleavened Bread, very near the time Jesus was to be executed on the cross, His disciples approached him and asked, "Where will you have us prepare for you to eat the Passover" (Matt 26:17)? Despite the fact that Jesus was facing imminent betrayal and death, his response to this question was void of panic or frustration.

> He said, "Go into the city to a certain man and say to him, 'The Teacher says, My time is at hand. I will keep the Passover at your house with my disciples.'" And the disciples did as Jesus had directed them, and they prepared the Passover. When it was evening, he reclined at table with the twelve (Matt 26:18-20)

Jesus' response is noteworthy because we often, when confronted with a question about future plans, become offended when such inquires appear to be questioning our initiative. At the very least, we typically find ourselves caught off guard because the question is about something we have not yet considered. "I don't know! I'm too busy," we might reply. "I don't really want to think about these things right now. I'd rather be doing something else." Jesus, however, was not offended by the question or caught off guard by it. Why? For the simple reason that He had already made plans for the Passover supper with His disciples. Jesus planned for the benefit of others. We see similar preparation by the apostle Paul in Romans 1:13-14, for example, where he indicates to the church at Rome that he *planned* to visit the church in order to bless them spiritually through the preaching of the gospel.

What this means, brothers, is that we are called by God to plan for the good of others. If you are in a romantic relationship, the burden lies upon you to direct the relationship in a Christ-honoring direction, whether it is planning dates or time together, or charting how you will discuss future plans, marriage, and other important issues. Certainly, your girlfriend will have a part in the direction of the relationship and will suggest and make plans as well. But we should feel the weight of failure and that our masculinity has been compromised if our girlfriends are handling the majority of the planning and leadership in our discussions.

Whenever I ask a Christian young man about the direction of his relationship with his girlfriend, I am often met with pious sounding language that centers around God's will. "Well, *if God wills*, then I would like us to get married someday." Or, "You know, we can't know the future, but *if the Lord wills* I could see myself marrying her." While this may appear as spiritual maturity, it is actually a pious-sounding guise for indecision and an unwillingness to make a commitment. While it is wise to humbly submit to God's *sovereign will of decree* and recognize that he ultimately in control of our futures (James 4:13-16), it is equally foolish to neglect God's *revealed will of desire* which makes it clear that the direction of the relationship and whether or not we get married is primarily up to us men.[4]

Similarly, if you are a husband or daddy, this means that you cannot leave all the family planning—how your family will conduct devotional time, handle discipline, spend money, go on vacations, etc.—to your wife. This does not mean that a wife cannot make plans for the family in these areas. Indeed, one of the joys of managing a home is overseeing the daily and monthly family schedules.

For example, my wife excels at planning and organization, and she is regularly planning fun outings for our family, creative ideas to weave Scripture memory and theology into the lives of our two boys, and time for us to spend alone together. But I have failed in my leadership if I become passive in the area of planning and leave it all to my wife. If I am going to fulfill my renewed Christian manhood, then I must courageously make plans for my family and take an active interest in what my wife is planning.

To Reconcile Broken Relationships

Fourth, men are responsible to take the initiative by reconciling broken relationships. We find the theological basis for this responsibility in the gospel, for it was Christ who sought reconciliation with His bride while she was still in rebellion against Him (see Rom 5:6-11). Christ made the first move toward healing the breach in our relationship with Him and provided everything required for true reconciliation. We did nothing but respond to his gracious call of reconciliation. Husbands are now called to model Christ in this way by loving their wives and laying their lives down for them (Eph 5:25). Christ laid down his life to reconcile His bride, and we must be willing to lay down our life—usually our pride and bruised ego—for the sake of reconciliation with our bride.

Practically, this means that husbands must lead in pursuing reconciliation in the relationship any time there is a breach of relationship. A mature man will feel the weight of this responsibility whenever there's relational trouble in the home, especially when he is to blame. But he will feel this weight even if the fault for the marital rupture belongs primarily to the wife. It is possible for a wife sin against her husband in a way that leaves him innocent of wrong. But even in such cases the Scripture places the obligation upon the man to, like Christ, make the first move of reconciliation. Again, this does not mean that the wife cannot and should not initiate forgiveness and restoration when there is a problem in the relationship with her husband. If she is a Christian, she is obligated by Scripture to pursue peace and reconciliation with her husband (see Matt 5:23-25; 18:15; Luke 17:3). But a man will compromise his masculinity if this direction of initiating reconciliation becomes a pattern and he is no longer taking an active role in healing the breach in his relationship with his wife.

For single men, I believe the responsibility to reconcile relationships with your sisters in Christ still resides upon you. Although marriage provides clear parameters within which to understand the dynamic of male and female relationships as they pertain to leadership, the creation order itself draws us to conclude that men generally bear the unique responsibility to take the initiative to solve relational problems. That is, there will be a strain upon the created order when men—at church, with their sisters and mothers, at work with female colleagues—passively allow women to be the primary initiators in healing broken relationships between themselves and other men.

To Make Decisions that Benefit Others

Mature manhood also takes the initiative to make decisions that benefit others. Many of us, however, are often indecisive on important issues because making a decision requires that we live with the consequences of that decision and risk the possibility of disagreement with others. Thankfully, Jesus gives us both the grace and the example to help us cultivate godly decisiveness. We see such an example as Jesus ministers to His disciples just prior to his death on the cross.

In John 13 we find the stirring narrative of Jesus humbly serving His disciples by washing their feet. The practice of washing feet, however, was typically reserved for the lowliest servants. Surely, Jesus would not stoop to such a level to wash the smelly, dirty feet of His disciples. Yet, stunningly, Jesus removes his outer garments, girds himself with the towel, pours water into a basin, and begins to wash the disciples' feet (John 13:4-5).

Peter, however, aware of the socially unacceptable event about to take place, rejects Jesus' initial attempt to wash his feet. "He came to Simon Peter, who said to him, 'Lord, do you wash my feet?'" (John 13:6). But Jesus does not circumvent or ignore Peter's objection. Rather, our wise and winsome Lord explained to Peter the reason for His actions in order to win his doubting disciple to His position. But Peter continues to object: "Jesus answered him, 'What I am doing you do not understand now, but afterward you will understand.' Peter said to him, 'You shall never wash my feet'" (John 13:7-8).

Yet, such resistance did not impede Jesus from following through with His decision to wash Peter's feet. Our Lord knew that it was good for Peter to receive his Master's foot-washing ministry, despite the social awkwardness of such a practice. What we see here is essential to our understanding of godly masculinity: Jesus was willing to make *an unpopular decision* for the good of those to whom He had been entrusted. But Jesus did not merely ram the decision through without first explaining to His disciples the purpose for actions. There were specific and very important purposes in Jesus' act of washing of the disciples' feet.

First, Jesus was providing His disciples with an earthy illustration of a spiritual reality. It was required of the disciples, if they were to truly have fellowship with Jesus, that they submit themselves to Jesus' cleansing of their hearts from sin. The washing of their feet symbolized their need to yield to Jesus' ministry *to them* before they rendered service *to Him* (John 13:8). Secondly, Jesus was supplying them with an example of how they were called to serve one another.

Once Jesus explained the reason behind His actions, Peter happily yielded to His plans. There is much wisdom here. Not only does this story imply that leaders must be willing to, at times, make unpopular decisions, it also teaches us that it is possible and preferable to *win* those with whom we've been entrusted to our side. If we are always making unpopular decisions or if we are constantly unable to win those under our care to embrace our decisions, then we are poor leaders who need to re-examine our source of wisdom and approach to leadership.

We also see in this episode that making decisions for the

good of others often requires self-sacrifice. Indeed, the entire plan of salvation that God initiated in eternity past was a self-sacrificial plan. God would give up His Son to death, and the Son would bear the punishment for sins He did not commit for the eternal benefit of His people. In the upper room, Jesus girds Himself like a lowly servant in order to serve those who had been entrusted to his leadership. Sometimes our decisions will be unpopular because we fail to adequately win others to our position. But sometimes our decisions will be unpopular because they are self-serving decisions that mainly benefit us. Christ shows us a better way. Men, if we are going to exercise godly masculinity, then overall flavor of our decisions should be one of self-sacrifice where we lay down our own lives for the sake of those we are leading.

Making decisions that benefit others also requires men to cultivate a sober mind (see Titus 2:2; 1 Pet 1:13; 4:7; 5:8). When we hear the phrase, "sober mind," we might think that Scripture is calling us give up fun and creativity and embrace a life of dull seriousness. Far from it. The Old and New Testament make it clear that godly manhood rarely, if ever, ends in dullness. Rather, sober-mindedness in relation to decision-making is vital because it enables us to think clearly about potential decisions and weigh our options without being tossed to and fro by the whims of emotion or circumstance.

Though not an evangelical Christian, George Washington exemplified this characteristic of sober-mindedness particularly well. In his book *1776*, David McCullough describes Washington's unique ability to set aside the vision-blurring effects of wishful thinking. Had we not known the outcome of the Revolutionary War, most of McCullough's historical narrative would have us wondering how the fledgling American colonies could possibly overcome the English military. Washington had endured multiple defeats on important battlefronts, and the possibility of American victory seemed to decrease with every passing winter month. Important decisions had to be made if victory was to be even a faint possibility, and these decisions needed the clear-eyed judgment of a man who drew on reality as it was, not what hoped it would be. "Seeing things as they were, not as he would wish they were," McCullough explains, "was known to be one of Washington's salient strengths."[5]

This descriptive sentence from McCullough illustrates well the character quality of sober-mindedness when it comes to making decisions. When confronted with trying circumstances, mature manhood makes decisions based on life as it really is and the appropriate biblical principles, not on wishful thinking or hope for a different situation.

To Draw on the Strengths of Others

Finally, mature manhood senses and assumes responsibility to lead by taking initiative to draw on the strengths of others. As we've already seen, one of the burdens of godly leadership is the responsibility for making decisions. That means, practically, that the husband bears the weight of making significant family decisions and living with the consequences of those decisions. What this does *not* mean, however, is that good leadership should be equated with unilateral decision-making.

For the first few years of our marriage, I held to the false notion that good leadership was gauged by how little input or advice a man received from his wife when making large-scale family decisions. As you would expect, this often led to conflict in our marriage, not because my wife craved my role as leader, but because I ended up making poor, ill-thought decisions! I believed, wrongly, that it was a threat to my leadership if I sought out wisdom from those around me, including those I was called to lead. How glad I was—and how happy my wife was—when I started to realize, from Scripture, that a feature of excellent leadership is its ability to exercise wisdom in drawing on the strengths of others. "A wise man listens to advice," Solomon reminds us (Prov 12:15).

As a woman, my wife has insights into life and church and relationships that I simply do not have. She has strengths that I do not possess. It is foolish in the extreme, therefore, to not consult these insights and access these strengths when making decisions. There are times when my wife has *better ideas* or *better solutions* than I do in certain circumstances. It is not weak leadership to utilize these ideas and solutions. On the contrary, it is a sign of strong, wise leadership when a man can listen to his wife's wisdom and incorporate her good ideas into the planning and decision-making process. Masculine immaturity breeds an unwillingness to listen to a woman's wisdom and insight. Mature masculinity gladly receives such insight and uses it for the benefit of those under his care.

And this principle applies to married *and* single men. Men should never feel threatened by the advice of another woman or be unwilling to seek it. That bit of insight she offers may be God's gift to you so that you can implement a plan superior to the one you were going to implement.

Implied in this call to make profitable use of the wisdom of other women is the responsibility of men to exalt the female gender. Godly men should be the *first* to praise the godly women in their midst and thank God for the blessing of femininity. What a glorious gift women are to our families, to our church, and to the world! Men should take their cues from the biblical authors at this point.

For example, although Scripture places the burden of leadership squarely upon the man, it is also careful to extol the beauty and goodness of the woman as she fulfills her role. Proverbs 31:10-31, while maintaining the woman's role as the one who nurtures new life and cares for the home, also tells us that the God-fearing woman is trustworthy (v. 11-12), hard-working (v. 13-15, 19), competent in finances (v. 16, 18, 24), physically strong (v. 17), generous to the poor (v. 20), devoted to the needs of her family (v. 21), sensible to aesthetic beauty (v. 22), and full of wisdom and kindness (v.25). Her character endows her inestimable worth (v. 10) and a well-deserved reputation (v. 23).

Luke extolls the godliness and faith of women regularly in his Gospel (Luke 1:26-38; 39-45; 46-56; 57-66; 2:36-38; 8:1-3), while the apostle Paul spoke highly of women as he labored alongside of them (Rom 16:3). Peter wrote of women whose character was precious to God (1 Peter 3:4) and who exercised courage in the face of frightening circumstances (1 Peter 3:6). Of course, our model is Jesus who treated women with respect and dignity even when such treatment was unpopular or socially unwarranted (see Luke 7:36-50; 13:10-17).

Conclusion

So godly masculinity takes the initiative to *lead* by setting the example, casting a biblical vision, planning for the good of others, reconciling broken relationships, making decisions that benefit those under his care, and by drawing strengths of others. This is a weighty burden that cannot be borne alone.

We need God to supply us with strength and wisdom to carry out our task. Happily, He has given us his Holy Spirit to enable us to fulfill our role as men (see John 14:16-17). As we move into these next few chapters to discuss the man's responsibility to protect and provide for those under his care, let's ask the Lord to help us depend upon Him as we take up this high calling to be the men He has re-created us to be.

4

The Calling of Mature Manhood: Protection

We saw in the last chapter that men are called to exercise leadership by taking the initiative in several crucial areas of life. In this chapter we are going to examine the second responsibility of mature manhood. Let's look again at our definition.

> Out of a heart of courageous love, mature manhood senses and assumes a God-given responsibility to lead, **protect**, and provide for those under his care, for their temporal and eternal benefit.

Again, like last chapter, it is important to say that a mature man senses *and* assumes his God-given responsibility to protect those under his care because there may be times when he is unable to assume this role of protector. Physical injury may hinder him, for example, from swiftly and decisively confronting an intruder in the home or assailant on the street. Or, a man may be away from his family on a business trip and not be immediately available to handle spiritual problems and fend off false teaching that the enemy has recently launched upon his family. In both cases, however, a godly man will sense a desire to exercise this kind of protection and find alternative ways to ensure his family's physical and spiritual safety when he is inhibited from doing so either bodily or geographically.

What Kind of Protection?

What I've already assumed in the previous paragraph is that there are two kinds of protection men are responsible to exercise among those whom God has entrusted to his care. The first, and what *should* be the most obvious is the call for physical protection. I say *"should* be the most obvious" because there are some today who teach that the notion that men are called to be the primary protectors of women is an outmoded social convention that smacks of the paternalism of a by-gone era. Women today have learned they must protect themselves and not depend upon the protection of men.

Because we live in a fallen world and people with violent, evil intentions lurk in the shadows in order to harm or take advantage of vulnerable women, it is right to encourage females to be vigilant and teach them how to protect themselves from potential enemies. But this affirmation of the importance of women protecting themselves does not undermine the fact that God has given men a unique responsibility to protect those around him, particularly women.

We noted in chapter one that Adam's responsibility was to "work and keep" the garden. The word "keep" (שָׁמַר; *shamar*) in Genesis 2:15 indicates that one of Adam's clear tasks was to *protect* the garden. This word is used often in the Old

Testament, and regularly with reference to a man's responsibility to guard another person. For example, after he spares Saul's life a second time, David rebukes Abner, Saul's military commander, for allowing him to come within striking distance of the king.

> Then David went over to the other side and stood far off on the top of the hill, with a great space between them. And David called to the army, and to Abner the son of Ner saying, "Will you not answer, Abner?" Then Abner answered, "Who are you who calls to the king?" And David said to Abner, "Are you not a man? Who is like you in Israel? Why have you not kept watch over your lord the king? For one of the people in to destroy the king your lord. This thing you have done is not good. As the LORD lives, you deserve to die, because you have not kept watch over your lord, the LORD's anointed (1 Sam 26:13-16).

In this passage, שָׁמַר (*shamar*) is used twice with the idea of "keeping watch" (for other examples of this usage, see 2 Sam 11:16; 18:12 Ps 121:7). The word also implies that this guarding will be exercised with diligence and watchfulness.

When God used this word to describe Adam's duties in the Garden of Eden, He was instructing the man to carefully and judiciously guard his new home from potential intruders. As the narrative unfolds, it becomes obvious that the man was responsible to protect the woman from enemies but that he had failed to do so. God told the man to guard the garden from evil intruders, but the skeptical, crafty serpent didn't get as much as a word of warning from Adam.

Nevertheless, as the biblical story progresses, we see that

men are those to whom the primary responsibility of protection is given. God establishes men in the role as judge and king for the military protection of Israel, and authoritative male prophets for the nation's spiritual protection. Although God used a woman to deliver Israel during the times of the judges (Judges 4-5) and spoke occasionally through prophetesses throughout Israel's history (Ex 15:20; Judg 4:4; 2 Kings 22:14; 2 Chron 34:22; Neh 6:14; Is 8:3), the pattern of men providing military and spiritual protection for the nation is essentially seamless throughout the Old Testament.

This pattern continues into the New Testament. As soon as we step into New Testament revelation we find that the man is the one to whom the duty of protection is given. In Matthew's birth narrative, for example, it is Joseph who is responsible for guiding his family safely out of the reach of the murderous king Herod.

> Now when [magi] had departed, behold, an angel of the Lord appeared to Joseph in a dream and said, "Rise, take the child and his mother, and flee to Egypt, and remain there until I tell you, for Herod is about to search for the child, to destroy him." And he rose and took the child and his mother by night and departed to Egypt and remained there until the death of Herod (Matt 2:13-15).

Why did God send His angel to Joseph instead of Mary in this case? A divine flip of a coin? No, it was fitting for God to choose Joseph to lead his family out of harm's way because from the beginning of creation the man has, by God's design, borne a unique responsibility to protect his family, particularly the women and children of his family.

With regard to spiritual protection we must note that although God speaks through women in the New Testament (see Luke 1:46-55; 1 Cor 11:5), it is the men to who God has entrusted the role of authoritative preacher, teacher, and overseer. That is why only men are allowed to fulfill the role of pastor-elder (1 Tim 3:1-7), preacher (1 Tim 4:1-3), and authoritative teacher (1 Tim 2:13-14; 1 Cor 14:26-40) in the church setting. In the home, men bear the responsibility to wash their wives with the water of the Word (Eph 5:26), which means nothing less than spiritually protecting them from that which is contrary to that Word. When these considerations are placed along the fact that only men were called as authors of Scripture and apostles of Christ, and that Paul instructs specifically the men at Corinth to be "Be watchful, stand firm in the faith [and] . . . be strong" (1 Cor 16:13), it becomes clear that both the Old and New Testaments lay upon the man a unique burden to protect women both physically and spiritually.

It's no wonder, then, why the New Testament often speaks of our spiritual struggle in military terms (see 2 Cor 10:4; Eph 6:10-18) and why, when referring to fellow soldiers in the battle, Paul only refers to other men (see Phil 2:25; 2 Tim 2:3-4; see also 1 Tim 1:18). This distinction between the roles of the man and the woman in this regard is brought out vividly in Paul's letter to Philemon when he addresses "Apphia *our sister* and Archippus *our fellow soldier*" (Philem 1:2, emphasis added).

Of course, none of this is meant to imply that a woman should neglect waging her own spiritual warfare for the sake of her children or friends or physically protecting the people she loves (see Eph 6:10-18). Everyone knows how quickly a mommy's protective instinct engages when the lives of her children are threatened. And there may be times when a woman will need to protect a man who is physically incapacitated and unable to wage any kind of self-defense toward an assailant. But Scripture makes it clear that it is the man who bears the unique responsibility to protect the woman, not the other way around.

Protecting the Women and Children in Our Life

Now that we have established the biblical foundation for our understanding of man's role as protector, what does this mean practically for us? Consider with me the following implications.

(1) A mature man will gladly and proactively protect the physical welfare of the women and children in his life

The obvious implication of what we have seen in Scripture is that mature manhood will be measured, in large part, by a man's willingness to protect those who have been entrusted to him. This means that a man must be willing to *take risks* to protect the women and children in his life. Courage, then, is essential to fulfill this calling, which is why we started chapter two with an exhortation to cultivate this vital spiritual virtue. The world is fallen, and, like it or not, there are people out there who desire to harm others. And their desire to harm others may, at some point, be directed at your family. If you are going to grow as a man, you must be willing to lay down your life to shield your loved ones from danger.

But what does it look like to protect others physically? It means, most literally, fending off attackers and those who seek to physically harm the vulnerable. It means embracing the "women and children first" rule and resisting the pull of self-protection. You may not consider yourself an athletic person, and you may not be someone who is particularly imposing; athletic prowess and size do not matter, however. Your manhood hangs on whether or not you will be the first to engage someone who attempts to harm your family. Nor does it matter whether or not your wife is superior to you in self-defense or martial arts. Our masculinity is expressed by taking the *initiative* to confront and subdue the aggressor. One author helpfully explains:

> It may be in any given instance of danger the woman will have the strength to strike the saving blow. It may be too that she will have the presence of mind to think of the best way of escape. It may be that she will fight tooth and claw to save a crippled man and lay down her life for him if necessary. But this does not diminish the unique call of manhood when he and his female companion are confronted by danger together. . . . A mature man senses instinctively that as a man he is called to take the lead in guarding the woman he is with.[1]

There may be times when a woman is more physically prepared to fend off an attacker because she is more fit or better at jiu-jitsu than the man. But a man will feel the God-given call to protect the woman he is with, not yield to her protection.

Men should also play an active role in protecting children. Godly men will sense a responsibility to make sure the children around them—in their home, their family, at church, at a park—are safe. I am not talking about how children play, specifically. Men are often more willing to let their kids and the kids around them play in ways that appear too risky for mom's comfort. Rather, I am referring to specific forms of child abuse perpetrated by older children or adults. Practically, men should be constantly aware of potential predatory threats, physical abuse, and kidnapping. Although women are often better at sensing when a child might be in danger or when someone is acting suspiciously around children, men cannot yield to passivity in this area. We must see ourselves as soldiers, called by our King to stand guard at the parameter of the palace so that those inside can live and play without fear.[2]

(2) A mature man will gladly and proactively protect the spiritual welfare of the women and children in his life

Unless a man is entirely bereft of healthy masculinity, he will mostly likely agree with the above exhortations, regardless of his religious commitments. Men are designed by God to protect the women and children around them. Christian men, however, will sense an additional responsibility. As we noted above, men who follow Christ will make it a priority to protect the women and children in their life from spiritual harm. And, given the nature of our task, we must apply Spirit-empowered diligence. "Men, spiritual warfare is not child's play," one author reminds us. "Satan is not simply seeking to injure your children—he is seeking to devour them."[3]

One of the ways we protect women and children in our life from spiritual harm is by we guarding them from false teaching. For husbands and dads, this means we take an active role in regularly praying for our family, gathering them together for devotional reading of Scripture, and keeping a careful eye on the influences that we allow into the home. A man should initiate spiritual and theological conversations with his wife and children and invest time into personal study so that he might have the intellectual tools with which to discern the possible threats to their spiritual health. Again, you may not consider yourself a scholar or much of a reader. But regardless of our personal inclinations or perceived strengths, our call to spiritually protect those under our care and in our sphere of influence *requires* that we give some time to personal study of Scripture and theology. Granted, this may mean you need to watch less television or set aside a few hobbies, but the sacrifice will pay rich dividends as you grow in the discernment and wisdom needed to guard those around you from spiritual harm.

Dads will also need to take an active role in determining what movies and television shows our children are allowed to watch, and what kind of access they should have to personal technology like smartphones, tablets, and computers. But if you think this last exhortation is overreaching and overbearing, you may not be fully aware of the role personal technology plays in influencing your children. Consider the following few issues.

Addiction to Unhealthy Stimuli
While I can say with a good conscience that I am grateful to God for how my iPhone and iPad have facilitated efficiency and productivity in my life, I am also fully aware of how easily it is to become addicted to certain forms of unhealthy stimuli produced by these two devices. But now that smart phones and tablets have been on the market for nearly ten years, we are able to draw from countless studies and form fairly consistent conclusions on the ways personal technology is changing us, for good and for ill.[4]

But we don't really need studies to confirm what we already know from experience. If we are honest with ourselves and our own hearts, we will have to admit that we sense an addictive craving for what our smart phone can offer us. Just ask yourself: how long do you typically go without looking at your smart phone? How long do your kids go? This growing addition for immediate sensory stimuli from images and entertainment is already having a detrimental effect on our child's brain development, ability to concentrate, and capacity to interact appropriately in social settings. Awareness of others is drowned by attachment to virtual interaction, and the mind is slowly numbed and inhibited from thinking clearly, connectedly, and carefully. A young Christian's taste for deep spiritual enjoyment will be muted by constant engagement with the trivial.[5] Men, wake up to how your children's devices are affecting them and take action. You cannot afford to be passive in this area.

Ease of Access to Pornography

But the above problems with regard our children's addiction to unhealthy stimuli pale in comparison with the danger of your child's access to pornography. Brothers, let me be plain: you should be more willing to take a bullet than for your son or daughter to view pornography even one time. Just one glimpse of pornographic material can lodge itself in the mind of a child for years and have enduring effects on how they view sexuality, their friends, the opposite sex, and their own bodies. If you think that you can slouch into your easy chair, turn on ESPN, and leave it to your child's discretion and wisdom to navigate their smartphone or tablet use, you will one day find out—I promise—how wrong you really were.

The Internet and the various apps available for

smartphones and tablets today are a virtual trove of pornographic material—from soft to hardcore pornography. Still images of naked men and women to videos of the actual sex act are only one or two clicks away from your child's eyes. Even among the more "innocent" apps, one can stumble upon all kinds of filth, often because the programmers and engineers tasked with guarding these apps from pornographic infiltration cannot keep up with all the material with which they are barraged twenty-four hours a day.

I am not telling you whether or not your teenager should own a smart phone or whether your child should be allowed to play games on a tablet. Rather, my point is to arrest your attention with these horrifying realities so that you will not be lulled to sleep by the enemy through indifference or ignorance. If you are going to protect your family, you must be willing to actively engage this area of technology.

Protecting Your Family's Sexual Purity
Men should also be active in protecting their family's sexual purity. This kind of protection, however, is not merely for your daughters. It is for your sons as well as your wife. Starting with the one whom God calls you to wash with the water of His Word, you must protect your wife's sexual purity by guarding her from unhelpful and unholy input. While your wife is responsible before the Lord to guard her own heart (Prov 4:29) and pursue holiness in obedience to Christ (Heb 12:14), you are responsible to help her in this area by not placing any stumbling blocks before her.

For example, you should exercise great caution with what movies or television shows you watch together. It is typically believed by most professing Christians that sexual images and scenes of sexual intimacy affect men more profoundly then women when it comes to their respective purity. While there is some truth to that claim, it is unwise and illegitimate to therefore conclude that such images *do not* affect women, or that it is acceptable before God for a wife to watch what, for moral reasons, her husband cannot. It is unhelpful to your wife's pursuit of holiness to expose her to movies and television that promote sexual immorality, and as men we should be willing to forego a particular movie or program for the sake of maintaining a clean conscience.

Regarding our sons, we should be making an effort, at a very early age, to promote sexual holiness around our boys. A wholesome view of sexuality will first come from how we treat our wives. It is good and wise for husbands to regularly express appropriate affection toward their wives in front of their children. Hugs, brief kisses on the cheek and lips, hand-holding, and gentle caressing, should be regular expressions of your love for your wife. Such expressions of love will serve to foster in your boys a healthy attitude toward sexuality and physical affection.

But in order for these displays of affection to be truly effective in your sons, they must be exclusive to your wife. In other words, our boys must see that we treat *only* their mother with that kind of affection. Flirtatious behavior and physically affectionate conduct toward other women—regardless of how you treat your wife—will only confuse your sons as to how they are to treat other women and think about marital intimacy.

Such commitment to your wife will also express itself in how you handle entertainment. Sure, you might keep your hands to yourself around other women, but your boys know what you are watching on T. V. or looking at on the Internet. It will be difficult to cultivate a healthy view of sexuality among your sons if are indulging in unwholesome television or surveying the women's magazines in the check-out line at the store.

Coupled with the dad's attention to his personal holiness will be deliberate talks—when the child is of appropriate age—about the beauty, goodness, and sacredness of sexual intimacy in marriage. It might sound intimidating to talk to your sons about sex, but this is a fear *you must* overcome by God's grace. If you do not, you will leave your son's sexual education primarily to the television, movies, magazines, and his peers; a frightening prospect for any dad who cares about his call to protect his family's sexual purity.

Concerning our daughters, we must be vigilant in protecting their purity as well. Practically, this means that dads should have a say in what their daughters wear and both encourage and require modesty in their girls as long as they are under his authority and care. Protecting our daughters' sexual purity will also require that we show them much physical affection as they grow from little girls into young women. A girl whose dad regularly expresses wholesome physical affection to her will be far less likely to seek such affection from other men and will be helped in her own fight for purity.

Finally, it should go without saying that dads should take an active role in vetting any young man who desires to date their daughters. I know that Christian families have different opinions about this particular topic, but I believe it is unwise for junior high-age children to become involved in dating relationships. Granted, junior high is the time when boys and girls are experiencing sexual maturity and transitioning from boys and girls to young men and women, and are beginning—perhaps for the first time—to feel genuine attraction toward members of the opposite sex. But it is precisely for this reason that parents should restrict their children from dating and should be, rather, using such a time to teach their children about the physical and emotional upheaval they are currently experiencing and help them navigate these new and often powerful desires for the opposite sex.

In my judgment it is naïve in the extreme for parents to allow their pre-teen and early teenage children to wade through this tumultuous time of sexual puberty without the steady guidance of godly, older wisdom. When the appropriate time comes, however, fathers should be ready to stand between their daughter and any potential suitor in order to allow access *only* to young men who have demonstrated genuine Christian character. I am not suggesting that a sixteen or eighteen or twenty year old man must possess the qualifications of an elder (see 1 Tim 3:1-7). But he must be a Christian and someone who is characterized by a reasonable amount of self-control (Titus 2:6).

I also think dads should require a personal conversation with a potential boyfriend before the young man is allowed to date his daughter in order to determine whether this particular young man is worthy of his daughter. The dad should also have specific rules already in place before the first date ever takes place (curfew, what kind of activities are appropriate, with whom his daughter and this young man will spend time, etc.). These kinds of rules will loosen in restriction as daughters increase in age, move out of the house, and become independent from their parents. Nevertheless, a dad should always desire to be involved at a significant level with his daughter's romantic life, offering guidance and protection, however that protection will take shape.

My goal in this section is not to provide an exhaustive treatise on how dads should fulfill their calling to protect their daughters. Rather, I simply want to highlight the importance of such a calling and encourage dads of young daughters to prepare well and men with older girls to take an active role in the lives of their daughters.

Protecting the Marriage Bed

For married men, the responsibility to guard the sexual relationship between his wife and himself is of utmost importance. Sexual intimacy between husband and wife is a precious gift, and God has given us this gift not only for our enjoyment, but in order to keep us from sexual temptation. Paul makes this very point in his first letter to the Corinthians.

> But because of sexual of the temptation to sexual immorality, each man should have his own wife, and each woman her own husband. The husband should give to his wife her conjugal rights, and likewise the wife to her husband. For the wife does not have authority over her own body, but the husband does. Likewise the husband does not have authority over his own body, but the wife does. Do not deprive one another, except perhaps by agreement for a limited time, that you may devote yourself to prayer, but then come together again, so that Satan may not tempt you because of your lack of self-control (1 Cor 7:2-5).

In this passage, Paul argues that defense against sexual temptation is bolstered by first entering into marriage, and then by engaging in regular sexual intimacy within marriage. Both the husband and the wife are to view the pleasure and enjoyment of their spouse as paramount, as each person freely offers himself or herself to the other. This free giving of oneself is what Paul means when he says, "For the wife does not have authority over her own body, but the husband does. Likewise the husband does not have authority over his own body, but the wife does." Paul is not suggesting that a man or a woman can do whatever they want to their spouse's body. Such a teaching would open the door for spousal abuse, and most often from the husband.

Rather, Paul is saying that each person should value the pleasure of their spouse in such a way that they give themselves to that enjoyment and therefore do not withhold sexual intimacy from their spouse. Paul makes his meaning clear when he adds, "Do not deprive one another." The temptation for a married couple will be to withhold sexual intercourse out of bitterness or in order to manipulate the other person. Some couples may even begin to conclude that too much sexual intimacy is a sign of spiritual immaturity, and only an occasional indulgence is to be preferred as the more "holy" practice. Paul demolishes this kind of thinking, and he charges both the husband and the wife to pursue regularly the pleasure of the marriage bed.

But although marital intimacy is one of God's greatest and most enjoyable gifts, there will be times within the marriage when a couple will be tempted to neglect this gift and fail to pursue it in the way it should be pursued. If you are a newly married couple, it might be difficult to imagine such a time in your marriage. Your passion for one another and the newness of your sexual union presently ensures your regularity in the marriage bed. And while the fire of sexual passion is essential and should be kindled regularly, there will be times that you are not as excited as you once were about engaging in sexual intercourse.

If one is primarily concerned about bringing delight to one's spouse and not merely securing satisfaction for himself or herself, for example, then one will find that sexual intimacy, though immensely pleasurable, requires work. Schedules, tiredness, the difficulties of child-rearing and other factors of regular life can also hinder a couple from coming together on a regular basis. Paul recognizes the hazard of sexual temptation gaining a foothold within the neglect of sexual intimacy, so he instructs the Christian couple to pursue regular, consistent sexual intimacy.

Protection in this area, therefore—as in every other area we have discussed—will require the man to *lead* and *take the initiative*. What do I mean? Practically, the husband must pursue sexual intimacy with his wife and not leave it to her initiative or to his mere feelings. Surprisingly, there may be times when you simply do not feel like having sex with your wife. Yes, hard to believe for some younger couples, but true nonetheless. Lack of affection isn't the issue, but work demands and disappointments, time-constraints, general weariness, and a hundred other factors will conspire to dampen your desire for marital intimacy and justify your resignation to passivity. It is at this point, however, that we must, by the power of the Holy Spirit, shun passivity and actively pursue our wives. As one author insightfully comments,

Sometimes sexual sloth comes from being busy with the wrong things. A guy who regularly works very long hours can actually be slothful if his choices about where to spend his time and energies leave not room for romancing his wife. How can hard work be sloth? Because a Christian husband is called to make sure he is regularly romancing his wife. If romance and intimacy are being pushed off the schedule too often, he needs to make what may be the more difficult decision: to set aside work and pursue his spouse.[6]

Laziness, therefore, is one of the chief enemies of sexual intimacy, and, by implication, a gateway for temptation to enter into the marriage. Shunning passivity at this point will also mean shunning passivity elsewhere in the marriage. A couple, for example, should never engage in sexual intimacy if they have unresolved conflict between each other. Sexual union during times of spiritual and relational disunity is a profound expression of hypocrisy, and will serve to undermine the relationship at a fundamental level. The husband, therefore, must take the initiative, as we saw in chapter two, to pursue reconciliation with his wife so that they might enter into physical intimacy with authenticity and a clean conscience. As in other areas, this call for men to take the initiative does not imply that the wife is unable to initiate sexual intimacy. She most certainly can, and she will bless her husband when she does. But something is amiss when the wife feels as though the burden is upon her to constantly initiate such times.[7]

Protecting Your Own Sexual Purity
Protecting the marriage bed also requires the husband to

protect his own sexual purity. The author of Hebrews makes a connection between honoring sexual intimacy within marriage and avoiding fornication and adultery: "Let marriage be held in honor among all, and let the marriage bed be undefiled, for God will judge the sexually immoral and adulterous" (Heb 13:4). Single men, therefore, have the responsibility to protect their marriage bed by avoiding sexual intimacy—fornication—with women who are not their wives. This means that men in dating relationships are called by God to treat their girlfriends and fiancés as someone else's wife until they make them their own wife. When a man fails to lead his girlfriend or fiancé into paths of sexual purity, he defiles the marriage bed and is in danger of God's judgment.

The married man must protect the marriage bed, as we've seen, by regularly pursuing his wife. But he also protects the marriage bed by steadfastly avoiding adultery. We learn from Jesus, however, that resisting adultery is more than just yielding to physical intercourse with another woman. It begins with the eyes and the heart. And so serious is this call to keep one's eyes and heart pure that Jesus threatens hell to those who carelessly indulge in lust.

> You have heard that it was said, "You shall not commit adultery." But I say to you that everyone who looks at a woman with lustful intent has already committed adultery with her in his heart. If your right eye causes you to sin, tear it out and throw it away. For it is better that you lose one of your members than that your whole body be thrown into hell. And if your right hand causes you to sin, cut it off and throw it away. For it is better that you lose one of your members than that

your whole body go into hell (Matt 5:27-30).

Jesus is not saying that a Christian who wrestles with lust will lose his salvation. Rather, He is saying that those who do not take lust seriously demonstrate that their faith is not saving faith, for saving faith wages eye-gouging, dismembering war on lust.[8] A life characterized by unchecked lust is a life headed for eternal hell. Protecting the marriage bed, therefore, requires that we rigorously avoid the mental adultery of lust. This admonishment is for married and single men.

Hard- and soft-core pornography, and all lesser forms of visual sexual stimulation, therefore, must be avoided at all costs. Gazing upon the body of a woman who is not your wife, or watching the depiction of the sex act devastates a man's heart and mind: sexual desire is perverted, healthy affections dampened, and masculine initiative curtailed. I believe one reason why male sexual-dysfunction drugs (e.g., Viagra) are so prevalent today is not because men lack the physical apparatus to engage in sexual intercourse, but because their minds have been ravaged by lust to the point where they require medical supplementation in order to become sexually aroused. Brothers, if we are constantly uninterested in sexual intimacy with our wives, this may well be a sign that we have not been careful to guard our eyes and hearts from mental adultery. Jesus said tear out an eye and cut off a hand in order to avoid lust.

That means do whatever it takes, even to the point where people will think you look strange, in order to avoid lust. You may not be able to watch certain movies or television programs. You may need to keep your head buried in the roster during the basketball game while the female dancers perform. You might need to get software for your computer and smartphone in order to protect yourself from illicit websites. You might need to get rid of the Internet altogether. Inconvenient? Perhaps. Potential fodder for ridicule from others? Maybe. But totally worth it in order to remain pure, go to heaven, and protect the marriage bed.

Single Men and the Call to Protect

Most of what I've said thus far applies most directly to husbands and dads. If you are a single man, several of these instructions are useful to help you prepare for marriage and fatherhood. But what about right now? And what if you are single for several years? Are you still called to protect others as a single man? The biblical answer is a resounding "Yes!" As we already noted, Jesus—a single man—serves as our example of how to protect others. He protected vulnerable women from the scorn and contempt of religious leaders (Luke 13:10-17). He protected His disciples from unlawful arrest and mistreatment (John 18:8). He protected children from unkind and unfair rejection (Luke 18:15-17). He protected people from the wiles of Satan and his demons (Luke 8:26-39). And He laid down His very life in order to protect us from the punishment that was due our sin (Rom 3:19-26; 6:23).

Single men, therefore, can have confidence in Christ that they can conduct a significant ministry of protection among their church and immediate family. For example, as I've already noted, men—married or not—should take an active interest in protecting the children at their church and in their families from sexual predators and those who intend them physical harm. Single men should see it as their calling to protect their sisters in Christ both physically and spiritually.

Sons should be ready to protect their mothers. Brothers should be prepared to protect their sisters and younger siblings. Adult grandchildren should count it a privilege to look out for their grandparents. Just take a moment to look around you: God has entrusted you with many, many opportunities for ministry, whether you are married or not. And you will find much joy and fulfillment as a man if you actively pursue these opportunities.

You are also called to protect the marriage bed, even though you are not yet married. You guard the marriage bed by protecting your own sexual purity, and by guarding your girlfriend or fiancé's sexual purity. Both of these duties require diligence, watchfulness, and courage. But the Spirit and the gifts are ours, and we are able, through Christ, to engage in the warfare of protection.[9]

Conclusion

If you are a man, then God has called and designed you to be a protector. If we neglect this calling, however, our masculinity will be compromised. We need courage, it's true. But God has already given us courage (2 Tim 1:7) and will enable us, as we depend on Him and act in faith, to fulfill this important duty of protection. He will also help us fulfill our calling to provide. It is to this issue we turn in chapter five.

5

The Calling of Mature Manhood: Provision

Having seen that men are called to lead and protect those under their care, we now turn to the third responsibility: provision. We look again to our definition of mature manhood.

> Out of a heart of courageous love, mature manhood senses and assumes a God-given responsibility to lead, protect, and **provide** for the temporal and eternal benefit of those under his care.

Like the first two responsibilities to lead and protect, this instruction is preceded by the qualification that mature manhood "senses and assumes" the duty to provide because there may be times when he is unable to provide for his family due to injury, health, or temporary unemployment. The man's ardent desire to provide, however, will remain, and he will do what he can to aid in this area of provision and probably wrestle with frustration when he is unable to do so. In such a case, a mature man who is unable to work will *sense* that it is his responsibility, although he will not be able to *assume* that responsibility.

Like the previous two responsibilities we discussed, the notion that men should be the primary providers for the family has come under attack in recent years. To suggest that men are given the unique responsibility to provide material sustenance to their families through their daily work is to bear witness that you are trapped in a past age of misogynic societal conventions that promoted, implicitly and explicitly, the oppression of women. Modern feminism, so the narrative goes, has freed us from such tyrannical thinking and enlightened us to the truth that women are just as competent as men to provide an income for the family, and should be given equal opportunity to work outside the home without hindrances of repressive cultural expectations. The idea that men are uniquely called and designed by God to provide for their families is a notion best kept in the dust bin of history.

While this is not the place to provide a full history and critique of the feminist movement in America, it is useful to note that not all women feel this way about the merits of feminism or the supposed repressiveness of traditional roles where the man provides for his family and the wife cares for the home and nurtures the children. Several women within the evangelical tradition have written extensively in order to defend the biblical view of men and women's roles and demonstrate the weaknesses of feminism.[1]

Nor is it my aim to question women's competence in comparison to men. When it comes to the ability to provide for her family, women have proven themselves over and over to be competent, highly-valuable employees and skillful entrepreneurs. In the case with single mothers, some women have no choice but to enter the workforce in order to provide for their children. The issue is not one of competence or ability, but of design and order. Scripture itself exalts female entrepreneurship and recognizes the worth of a woman who earns income for her family (see Prov 31:16-18, 24). But Scripture also teaches us that God has designed the man and the woman to fulfill specific roles and responsibilities that correspond to our respective genders. We noted some of these important distinctions between the man and the woman in chapter one as we walked through the narrative of Genesis 2-3. I want to revisit Genesis 3, but this time with special attention on what God did after Adam and Eve sinned.

Immediately after God confronted Adam and Eve, He made a promise of redemption: from Eve's offspring would come a man who would destroy the serpent (Gen 3:15). What the serpent did by tempting Adam and Eve, and what the couple had done by disobeying God would someday be undone. But after offering His first couple with this profound encouragement, God leveled them with the curse.

This curse would affect the man and the woman differently. But it is *how* the curse would affect the man and woman respectively that is particularly instructive. As we will see, God cursed the man and the woman *with respect to their roles*. Notice first God's words to Eve and then to Adam:

To the woman He said,

"I will surely multiply your pain in child-bearing;
in pain you shall bring forth children.

Your desire shall be contrary to your husband,
and he shall rule over you."

And to Adam He said,

"Because you have listened to the voice of your wife, and have eaten the tree of which I commanded you, "You shall not eat of it," cursed is the ground because of you; in pain you shall eat of it all the days of your life; thorns and thistles it shall bring forth for you; and you shall eat the plants of the field. By the sweat of your face you shall eat bread, till you return to the ground; for out of it you were taken, for you are dust, and to dust you shall return" (Gen 3:16-19).

Eve would experience the curse in her specific calling to bring new life into the world. Adam, however, would endure God's curse in the sphere of his calling to bring forth bread and produce from the ground. One might argue that the curse upon the ground will be Eve's to bear as well. Therefore, we don't have warrant to draw conclusions about male and female roles from this passage. While it is true that Eve would, in some measure, experience the "thorns and thistles" of daily existence in a cursed earth, what we must notice is that each curse was intended to touch upon the uniqueness of the man and woman's respective roles. Only the woman, for example, is able to bring forth new life. The man is biologically and physiologically unable to bear and birth children. The woman's calling to bring forth new life is unique to her as a woman. The man's calling to bring forth bread and produce from the ground is unique to his calling as a man.

Notice the parallel language between these two curses (emphasis added):

To the woman He said,

"I will surely multiply your pain in child-bearing; *in pain* you shall *bring forth* children.

Your desire shall be contrary to your husband, and he shall rule over you."

And to Adam He said,

"Because you have listened to the voice of your wife, and have eaten the tree of which I commanded you, 'You shall not eat of it,' cursed is the ground because of you; *in pain* you shall eat of it all the days of your life; thorns and thistles it shall *bring forth* for you; and you shall eat the plants of the field."

First we see the announcement of the curse. For Eve, God would multiply her pain in child-bearing. For Adam, God would curse the ground. Second, God explains how they would each experience the curse. In both cases, Adam and Eve will *bring forth* the fruit of their labor *in pain*. As one author explains,

When God creates the first human beings, he commands them to "be fruitful and multiply" (Gen. 1:28) and builds into them unique characteristics to carry out this task. The Creator designs the woman to bring forth and nurture offspring. Her name, Eve, means, the Scriptures tell us, "the mother of all living" (Gen. 3:20). The cosmic curse that comes upon the creation shows up, for the woman in the pain through which she carries out this calling—birth pangs (Gen. 3:16). The man, as the first human father, is "to work the ground from which he was taken" (Gen. 3:23). Adam, made of the earth, is to bring forth bread from the earth, a calling that is also frustrated by the curse. In this, Adam images a Father who protects and provides for his children.[2]

These parallels highlight that God had cursed Adam and Eve according to their particular, God-designed roles as man and woman. While it is true that the woman did not have similar restrictions when it came to producing bread from the ground—she is biologically and physiologically able to perform such tasks—it seems most plausible to see God's assignment of the curse as relating specifically to roles that were unique to Adam and Eve's respective manhood and womanhood. The remaining biblical narrative will affirm this interpretation, particularly the New Testament.

For example, we find in Paul's letters a consistent pattern of instruction regarding how men and women roles differ according to what we just saw in Genesis 3:16-19. In his first letter to Timothy, Paul provides his young pastor with a detailed plan of how the church should care for widows. Older widows were to look first to their family for support so that the church can avoid needless financial burdens. Such an arrangement pleases God and corresponds with His commandment for children to honor their parents (1 Tim 5:3-4 cf. Ex 20:12).

But if a widow meets certain criteria—she is older than sixty and has a reputation for godliness—the church is obligated to provide for her material needs. Younger widows, however, are not to be enrolled in the church's widow-support program. The reason for this restriction is because a widow without children who receives financial support from the church will be tempted toward idleness, gossip, and conducting herself as a busybody (1 Tim 5:13).

What is Paul's solution to this potential problem? "So I would have younger widows marry, bear children, manage their households, and give the adversary no occasion for slander" (1 Tim 5:14). In order to avoid a slothful, unprofitable lifestyle, Paul would have the young widows in the congregation marry, bear children, and manage their household. For the woman to pursue these activities is for her to walk in step with her God-given design. Paul gives similar instruction in his letter to Titus, in which he offers some important instruction on discipleship within the church.

> Older women likewise are to be reverent in behavior, not slanderers, or slaves to much wine. They are to teach what is good, and so train the young women to love their husbands and children, to be self-controlled, pure, working at home, kind, and submissive to their husbands, that the word of God may not be reviled (Titus 2:3-5).

The content of the older women's instruction to the younger women should be, among other things, specific guidance on how to love one's husband and children, and work profitably at home.[3]

But if we go back to Paul's instruction concerning the older widows who can receive provision from her children and grandchildren, we will find the man and his role mentioned in the passage in the context of a stern warning. Paul says, "But if anyone does not provide for his relatives, and especially for members of his household, he has denied the faith and is worse than an unbeliever" (1 Tim 5:8). To whom is Paul talking with this statement? He is speaking to those adult children who have mothers or grandmothers who are dependent upon them for material provision (v. 4). If these children or grandchildren do not supply their widowed mother or grandmother with what she needs, these men have "denied the faith and are worse than an unbeliever." Why such a serious charge? Because even unbelievers know intuitively that it is a healthy adult child's responsibility to provide for his parents and grandparents.

What is most interesting in this passage concerning our discussion of men and women's roles is that Paul addresses the man when he levels his warning about not providing for one's widowed mother or grandmother. "If anyone does not provide for *his* relatives, and especially for members of *his* household, *he* has denied the faith and is worse than an unbeliever" (1 Tim 5:8, emphasis added). To Paul, the distinction in roles between the man and the woman with regard to provision was clear. Such a distinction is seen elsewhere in Paul's writings.

In his second letter to the Thessalonians, for example, Paul rebukes strongly those who have, in their supposed zeal for spiritual things, neglected their duty to work for a living.

> Now we command you, brothers, in the name of our Lord Jesus Christ, that you keep away from any brother who is walking in idleness and not in accord with the tradition that you received from us. For you yourselves know how you ought to imitate us, because we were not idle when we were with you, nor did we eat anyone's bread without

paying for it, but with toil and labor we worked night and day, that we might not be a burden to any of you. It was not because we do not have that right, but to give you in ourselves an example to imitate. For even when we were with you, we would give you this command: If anyone is not willing to work, let him not eat. For we hear that some among you walk in idleness, not busy at work, but busybodies. Now such persons we command and encourage in the Lord Jesus Christ to do their work quietly and to earn their own living. As for you, brothers, do not grow weary in doing good. If anyone does not obey what we say in this letter, take note of that person, and have nothing to do with him, that he may be ashamed. Do not regard him as an enemy, but warn him as a brother (2 Thess 3:6-15).

Drawing from his own example of hard work and his refusal to financially burden anyone in Thessalonica, Paul instructs those who have neglected work to turn from their laziness and "work quietly and to earn their own living" (2 Thess 3:12). Notice, however, the nouns and pronouns Paul uses throughout his admonishment: "If anyone is not willing to work, let *him* not eat. . . . If anyone does not obey what we say in this letter, take note of that person, and have nothing to do with *him*, that *he* may be ashamed. Do not regard *him* as an enemy, but warn *him* as a *brother*" (2 Thess 3:10, 13-15). While it is likely that there would have been single women in this congregation who needed to hear this admonishment to labor productively for one's sustenance, the instruction is aimed primarily at the brothers at this church, I would argue, because Paul recognizes that men have been uniquely designed and called by God to work and bring forth food from the ground (see Gen 3:17-19).

There is also an important parallel to note between this passage and the passage in 1 Timothy 5:13-14. In the case of younger widows, Paul helps them avoid idleness and gossip by pursuing marriage and attending to the home and children. Similarly, Paul would have the men in Thessalonica avoid idleness and a lifestyle characterized by useless meddling by attending to profitable work (2 Thess 3:11). In other words, a woman avoids the snare of laziness when she attends to her calling as a woman (managing the home and children) and the man avoids the snare of laziness when he attends to his calling as a man (working to provide).

The calling for a man to provide for his family is brought into even sharper focus in Ephesians 5:25-33.

> Husbands, love your wives, as Christ loved the church and gave himself up for her, that he might sanctify her, having cleansed her by the washing of water with the word, so that he might present the church to himself in splendor, without spot or wrinkle or any such thing, that she might be holy and without blemish. In the same way husbands should love their wives as their own bodies. He who loves his wife loves himself. For no one ever hated his own flesh, but nourishes and cherishes it, just as Christ does the church, because we are members of his body. "Therefore a man shall leave his father and mother and hold fast to his wife, and the two shall become one flesh." This mystery is profound, and I am saying that it refers to Christ

and the church. However, let each one of you love his wife as himself, and let the wife see that she respects her husband.

According to this glorious passage of Scripture, a husband's calling by God is to love his wife as Christ loves His church. And how does Christ love His Church? By laying down His life for her and by pursuing her holiness by washing her with the water of the Word. In the same way, Paul tells us, men are to love their wives as their own bodies. Why? Because according to this passage and the passage in Genesis it references, the woman *is* his own body. The man and his wife are "one flesh," and it is obvious no one neglects or fails to care for his own body. It only makes sense, then, that the husband would nourish and cherish his wife.

The word "nourish" is particularly significant for our present discussion. This word, ἐκτρέφει (*ektrephei*) is used throughout the Septuagint and the New Testament to refer to rearing children (see Eph 6:4). But it also refers specifically to supplying another's physical needs.[4] Note how the word is used in the story of Joseph:

> **Genesis 45:11:** [In the land of Goshen] I will *provide* for you, for there are yet five years of famine to come, so that you and your household, and all that you have, do not come to poverty.

> **Genesis 47:17:** So they brought their livestock to Joseph, and Joseph gave them food in exchange for the horses, the flocks, the herds, and the donkeys. He *supplied* them with food in exchange for all their livestock that year.

Given these uses, therefore, we are able to conclude that Paul's intent in Ephesians 5:29 is to instruct the Christian men to provide for their wives just like Christ provides for his wife: spiritually *and* physically. While it is true that the call to nourish one's wife includes more than physical provision, it can never, for able-bodied men, include less. Indeed, Paul has already told us in 1 Timothy 5:8 that a man's supposed spirituality is called into serious question if he refuses to provide material sustenance for his family. After his own study of this passage and the word "nourish," on author helpfully concludes, "So the point is at least that the husband who leads like Christ takes the initiative to see to it that the needs of his wife and children are met. He provides for them."[5] A man's masculinity hangs on whether or not we will take up the responsibility to provide the material needs of his family.

A recent and growing phenomenon in America, however, is the "stay-at-home dad."[6] For various reasons—temporary unemployment, a wife's superior education and ability to earn income, the perceived domestic strengths of a particular husband and wife, or out of love for the other spouse—more men than ever are exchanging their role as provider for a role as homemaker and nurturer. But is this practice acceptable for Christians?

As I've already noted at the beginning of this chapter, there may be seasons when a wife will need to fulfill the role of provider. A man may be injured or unable to find a job and therefore unable to provide in the way he would like. For the sake of the family, he will yield to the wife's ability to earn income for the family. But he should *desire* to return to his role as soon as possible. Why? Because God has designed him to carry out his calling as a man, not as homemaker and nurturer, but as the one who provides for his family.

Given what we've seen in Scripture, we must conclude that it is entirely unfitting for an able-bodied man to be dependent upon his wife for physical provision, regardless of circumstances. In a home without children, it should go without saying that a man should work, irrespective of how much his wife makes (see 2 Thess 3:6-14). When children arrive, Scripture does not restrict entirely the woman from working, but it does make it clear that her priority is to care for the home and her children, and that her labor for provision should honor and facilitate these priorities. The Scripture, however, never relieves the man from his duty to provide.

What About a Couple's Perceived Strengths and Weaknesses?

Occasionally I will hear couples argue for the "stay-at-home dad" position from the perspective of the respective strengths and weaknesses him and his wife. The argument usually goes this way. "I am better at caring for children than my wife is, and as it turns out, my wife is better than me at earning income. Wisdom would compel us, therefore, to flip these traditional roles for the sake of our family."

While I might grant that there are cases where a man may possess—due to his upbringing, education, and general interests—a greater initial capacity than his wife to care for children, I do not believe a man's alleged superior parenting ability can ultimately surpass the woman's ability to care for children and the home. The woman may feel or actually be deficient in the area of child rearing and homemaking, but if what we have learned about God's design is true, then her weakness in this area—as well as her husband's strength—is

91

only superficial. Because her capacity to care for children is fundamental to her very personhood and design from God, then her diligence in this area will lead to genuine growth and she will soon surpass her husband as nurturer and homemaker.

What About Income Earning Ability?

Another argument for the stay-at-home dad position comes from an economic perspective. If the wife is able to earn more than the man, then it seems financially foolish to maintain traditional roles. Individual financial scenarios notwithstanding, this kind of argument typically reveals a man and woman's priorities. If it is true that God has designed man and woman for different roles, and that He calls us to live within these roles for His glory and our good, then to suggest that we should reverse these roles for the sake of more money shows us immediately what our heart really values. Often, couples have become attached to a certain lifestyle so they are unwilling, when children arrive, to take a step down financially in order to fulfill God's calling on their lives. In order to ease the conscience, a couple might even appeal to wisdom for their decision, claiming that they need to plan for the future.

This is one reason why my wife and I counsel young couples to live only off of the husband's income when they are first married. This practice makes it much easier for the couple to give up the woman's income once children enter the picture. If couples develop a lifestyle that is based on a dual income, it will be very difficult for them to forego a second income when children come along.

While I am not suggesting that families in this situation all-of-a-sudden upend their family structure, I am saying that in light of what we've studied, we must be willing to obey the Lord and trust Him to provide for us. We may not be able to afford the home, cars, and vacations we could otherwise afford, but we will be walking in obedience to Christ, and that's better anyway.

What About Love?

Some stay-at-home dads may appeal to love in their decision to stay at home with their children while their wife works. The argument usually goes like this: "I love my wife and value her happiness. Because she enjoys and finds fulfillment in her job, I want to give her this gift to enjoy by staying at home with the children while she pursues her career."

I certainly do not want to chide men who esteem their wife's happiness and who seek creative ways to express love to their wives. May more and more men grow in active and attentive love toward their wives! But it is possible to believe that we are expressing love toward our wives when we are, in fact, inhibiting them from what actually best serves their happiness. We are fallen, and our minds and hearts are easily led astray from what is right and good. Love is not enough. We need to learn how to love, and what true love looks like. That is why Paul prays the way he does for the Philippian church.

> And it is my prayer that your love may abound more and more, with knowledge and all discernment, so that you may approve what is excellent, and so be pure and blameless for the day of Christ, filled with the fruit of righteousness that comes through Jesus Christ, to the glory and praise of God (Phil 1:9-11).

Paul desires that our love abound, not as a mere feeling, but as a godly affection guided by knowledge and discernment. Accordingly, only when our love is led by knowledge and discernment will we be able to approve what is excellent, be filled with the fruit of righteousness, and, therefore be pure and blameless in the day of Christ. Said negatively: If we do not grow in knowledge and discernment, we run the risk of approving what is actually unworthy of praise and inhibits our practical righteousness.

While I don't doubt the sincerity of the men who say they stay at home out of love, I do question the spiritual maturity of this kind of love. If a woman has been designed and called by God to bring forth children, care for them, and manage the home, it may *feel* like self-sacrificial love for the man to relinquish his role as provider, but it is ultimately an act of unkindness, and therefore not true love (see 1 Cor 13:4). Nor does it qualify as Christlike love because it is not acting according to what is true (see 1 Cor 13:6). Rather than surrendering his role as provider, self-sacrificial love in this case would probably be expressed in a man's willingness to have some very difficult discussions with his wife about God's design and how, in the long run, the wife's yielding to God's call on her life for His glory will lead to her greater happiness. This kind of love will require the man to exercise courage and to be willing to make an initially unpopular decision for the good of his family. That's real love. It may not feel like it right away, but the Spirit is faithful to warm our affections as we walk in the truth.

Provision and the Single Man

For the single man, this inherent calling and sense to provide for women will not presently find an outlet in providing for a wife and children. An important question, then, is how does a single man fulfill this calling? Here are a few ideas. First, you may have a mother or grandmother or a sister who needs help financially (see 1 Tim 5:3-4). It might be the case that God has called you to fulfill your calling to provide by caring for your relatives. Second, you can give to your local church generally, but also specifically to a benevolence fund or widow's fund if one is available. Third, when going out to a meal with a group of ladies, you can offer to pay for the women's meals. Fourth, if there are single mothers in a local congregation, you may sense a desire to help provide for her in a way that is fitting and appropriate. Finally, it is the calling of all Christians to work to provide not only for themselves, but for those in need (see Eph 4:28). Single men, therefore, have the opportunity to provide for countless needs in their church and wider community. These are just a few ideas, but they demonstrate that it is possible and desirable for a single man to fulfill his calling to provide, even if he is not providing for a wife and children.

Conclusion

We have seen in the last few chapters what it means to grow in mature manhood. God calls us to courageously exercise leadership, to protect the vulnerable, and to provide for others. This is a heavy burden to bear. And if we attempt to bear it apart from the gospel, our leadership, protection, and provision will be bereft of humility and love.

Everyday, therefore, we must remind ourselves of the glorious truth that Christ Jesus has fulfilled every aspect of biblical manhood perfectly in our place. We do not lead, protect, and provide in order to get right with God or to make Him love us. We already have all of His favor through

Christ. His love for us is immovable, and we are secure in Him. God has designed that we fulfill these massive commands from the security of our salvation, not for it. And when we fail—and we often will—the gospel supplies us with hope for the future. We have a loving Father who is ready to forgive our sins, pick us up, and place us back on the path of godly manhood. When we refresh our minds regularly in the good news of God's love to us through Christ, we will be able to say along with John, that God's commandments are not burdensome (1 John 5:3) and with our Savior, that His yoke is easy (Matt 11:30).

6

On Leaving Father and Mother

Over the past three decades, our nation has seen a significant increase in the number of men living with their parents well into their mid- to late-twenties, and even early thirties.[1] Sociologists have traced this phenomenon to several causes: relative education, socio-economic factors, and our culture's general shift in expectations for men. The Church has also felt the effect of this turn in our nation's culture. Christian men are living with their parents for much longer than was previously seen as acceptable, and they are waiting longer than in times past to get married.

While some social commentators may view this as a harmless development, or, at least, something that is pragmatically acceptable for our current economic situation where jobs are difficult to find and homes hard to afford, Christian men cannot endorse this approach to manhood. Why? Because to do so would be to reject one of the primary aspects of our design as men.

A Man Shall Leave Father and Mother

Returning again to Genesis 2:24, we find that immediately after God creates Adam and Eve, Moses reflects on the present reality of manhood and marriage (at his time) and makes this observation:

> Therefore a man shall leave his father and his
> mother and hold fast to his wife, and they shall
> become one flesh.

The word "therefore" tells us that Moses is building his observation about the present state of manhood and marriage on his previous statements. In verses 22 and 23, Moses describes the creation of the woman from the man's side and God's presentation of the woman to Adam. "Therefore" or "for this reason,"—namely, the fact that God created the woman from the man—a man shall leave his father and his mother and cleave to his wife, and they shall become one flesh. In order for the man and the woman to be joined as one flesh as husband and wife, the relationship with their parents must change fundamentally: the children must *leave* their parents in order to *cleave* to each other.

The word Moses uses here for *leave* is a strong word. In other contexts it can mean "forsake" even "abandon." We know from how God addresses a child's relation to parents later in the biblical narrative that Moses does not mean *utterly* forsake or abandon. Adult children are still called to honor their parents (Ex 20:12; Deut 5:16), which implies a continuing relationship and concern for their welfare (note Jesus' comments on this passage in Matt 15:1-9). Nevertheless, by using this word Moses means to communicate that the relationship between these two children and their parents has changed in a basic, fundamental way. Structurally and ontologically, the relationship is different. No longer are these children under their parent's authority, supervision, or provision. They now make their own decisions pertaining to their individual lives and their life as a married couple. They are responsible to provide for themselves financially, and, while they may seek the counsel and wisdom of their parents, they are no longer under the obligation of obedience that characterized their relationship as young children.

But we are getting a little ahead of ourselves. I have been speaking with specific reference to a married couple and how they are to come together as one flesh in the context of leaving their individual parents. With respect specifically to our discussion of manhood, two important observations must be noted in this text. The first is an observation we already noted in chapter one: Moses directly addresses the man but only indirectly addresses the woman. "For this reason *a man* shall leave his father and mother and cleave to his wife and the two shall become one flesh" (Gen 2:24). It is the man who is leaving and cleaving to his wife. Why? Because if the man does not lead his bride to walk in accordance with the new one-flesh reality that has been forged by marriage, it will never happen.

Moses probably already sensed among God's people that passivity was a character trait that abounded among the men of Israel. Men are tempted, in the face of intimidating responsibility, unhealthy financial dependence on parents, and a host of other factors, to fail to leave their parents. The men in Israel needed to be reminded of their calling to lead their new family to live in accordance with God's design. But there's another observation that is often missed in this passage, and it is one that has become even more clear to me as a result of serving as an elder and shepherd in the local church.

As I've had the opportunity talk intentionally with young men about their relationship with their parents, I have learned of situations where parents still hold significant emotional sway over their adult sons and expect to be party to their major decisions, including career decisions and romantic interests. Yes, these men may have graduated from college and may now be pursuing jobs many miles from their families, but vocational status and geographical distance have not deterred these parents from assuming that it is their calling as parents to direct their son's life. In a few cases, I have been surprised to discover that these parents agree in the principle of leaving and cleaving, but the believe this event occurs *at* marriage, not prior to it.

These conversations have made it clear to me that the failure to make one small observation in Genesis 2:24 will have massive practical implications in the lives of Christian parents and their adult children. The parents of these young men have mistakenly concluded that leaving and cleaving are one-in-the-same event: that a man does not leave *until he cleaves*. But this is to misunderstand Moses' statement. Cleaving doesn't create the leaving, just like beginning to work at new job doesn't necessarily imply that you have left your old one. Rather, leaving comes prior to and creates the environment in which cleaving can actually occur. In other words, a man must first leave his parents *before* he can cleave to his wife. Leaving father and mother, therefore, occurs prior to marriage and is the necessary pre-requisite for it.

There are many grown Christian men who have yet to leave their father and mother and, for this reason, are not yet ready to be married. In many ways they are even disabled from pursuing marriage because they have not obeyed the calling to leave their parents. Some men may not even realize that they are still clinging to their parents in unhealthy ways so they are unable to diagnose their problem or even recognize that there is one. How does this failure to leave parents manifest itself in the life of a young man? I will suggest three ways.

(1) Dependence on Parents for Day-to-Day Expenses

As I noted in chapter five, it is the calling of all Christians—men especially—to provide for themselves. Young men who refuse to make their own way in the world by earning their own living and providing for their day-to-day expenses are compromising their manhood and have not yet left father and mother. This point certainly has implications for how long after college a man should live at home. I do not want to make any rules where Scripture is silent, and I am sure there are legitimate exceptions, but it seems fitting that once a man has been equipped to earn a living through college or technical school, he should leave the comfort of his parent's provision and earn his own living. Yes, it will be tough to make ends meet, and yes, you will need to make sacrifices, forego certain forms of entertainment, and work a lot. But these are God's tough yet wise means of spiritual maturity, and if you resist them in order to remain comfortable with mommy and daddy, you are regressing into childhood, not growing into manhood.

(2) Dependence on Parents for Major Decision-Making

Just as serious but perhaps less perceptible is a man's reliance on his parents for help in making major decisions. An adult man who honors and respects his parents will look to them for wisdom when faced with important decisions. That's natural. But if a young man is not branching out to find other counselors in his life, particularly older men and women within the church, but rather is guided chiefly by the opinions of his parents, he has yet to leave father and mother. A man's parents may know him well, but once he has left the home, there are other people—pastors, brothers in Christ, mentors, employers—who will know him better in some areas than even his own parents. This means that a man may make decisions that do not align with the wishes or counsel of his parents.

I am not talking about obvious sin issues, where to go against parental counsel is to violate clear biblical commands. The biblical counsel of parents should always remain tethered to the heart of Christian children into adulthood (see Prov 3:1-4). Rather, I am referring to matters like life-direction, romance, where to live, future employment, and how to navigate one's relationships. No longer should parents hold sole authoritative sway in a young man's life over these kinds of issues once he has left the home. God has designed that as he grows the man will carve out other channels of counsel so that he might make decisions that accord best with God's will. Scripture teaches that there is wisdom in a multitude of counselors (see Prov 11:14; 15:22). Limiting oneself to a single source of guidance, therefore, may prove detrimental to a man in the long term. While I know some godly parents who are able to think objectively about their son's potential decisions and point him in a biblical direction irrespective of their own desires, more often, parents—even the most faithful—are tempted to counsel their sons in ways that accord with *their* hopes and dreams rather than encouraging them to follow the Lord, wherever He may take them.

(3) Dependence on Parents for Emotional Approval
Similarly, a man has not yet fully left father and mother if he is reliant upon his parent's approval for his major decisions. If a man is constantly making decisions that accord *only* with his parents' wishes and counsel, it is likely that he is

emotionally dependent upon his parents to approve what he does. Again, when we are talking about a Christian young man with godly parents, a man's major life-decisions may often correspond with his parents' desires. But if he is *unable* to make decisions without garnering the approval of his parents, he has not yet left father and mother. I fear that many Christian young men are not fulfilling their full potential in work, ministry, or family life because they are unable to venture out into the world on their own. They may have moved out of the house, but their heart is still wrapped around their mom and dad for comfort, support, and approval. Until a man is able to move this dependence away from his parents and onto Christ and the Church, he has not fully left father and mother.

Leaving: More than Preparing for Marriage

So, leaving father and mother is about more than preparing for marriage, although it is a necessary prerequisite to marriage. In order to become the men God desires us to be, we must leave father and mother. For some men, fully leaving father and mother is difficult. There are situations where a man's parents may not have raised him to eventually leave; they never actively sought to equip and encourage their son to embrace the challenge of living on his own, earning all of his living, and making difficult decisions without the safety net of mom and dad's authoritative pronouncements. He is crippled from making progress in his life because his parents have, though probably out of good intentions, hindered his maturity and stunted his manhood.

If you recognize yourself in this description, you might begin to feel cheated, as though your parents have wronged you in the way they brought you up. I urge you: please confess your grief to the Lord and have mercy on your parents. We all stumble in many ways, and no parent is perfect. Besides, drudging up old alleged hurts is never the way forward. Rather than blaming your parents, begin to take strides, with the help of your church family, to becoming the man God has called you to be. You will probably need to have some difficult conversations with your parents as you express to them your desire to venture out from their protection and provision and remind them that it is God's design that you do so.

For other men, leaving will be and has been relatively easy. Not only have they been raised to leave the nest; they were gently nudged when the time came and they embraced the excitement of life away from home and parental protection and provision. Still others are naturally more eager to leave father and mother and make their way in the world. They look forward to moving away, making their own decisions, landing their own job, finding their own church, and earning their own living. These young men need to guard against the temptation to forget their parents (Prov 23:22) and be reminded that they will *always* have a responsibility to honor their parents (see Matt 15:1-9). But for the Christian, these obligations to one's parents are now dependent on a more important obligation.

Following Jesus and Honoring Parents

When Jesus instructs His followers on how to prioritize family relationships, He draws a sharp line of loyalty between Himself and man's family. In fact, some of Jesus' most startling statements are the ones He makes about family relationships in light of the kingdom of God. For example, in Matthew's gospel, Jesus claims that one of the very reasons

He came to earth was to bring division among one's closest relations.

> Do not think that I have come to bring peace to the earth. I have not come to bring peace, but a sword. For I have come to set a man against his father, and a daughter against her mother, and a daughter-in-law against her mother-in-law. And a person's enemies will be those of his own household. Whoever loves father or mother more than me is not worthy of me, and whoever loves son or daughter more than me is not worthy of me. And whoever does not take his cross and follow me is not worthy of me. Whoever finds his life will lose it, and whoever loses his life for my sake will find it (Matt 10:34-39).

To what is Jesus calling His disciples with these difficult words? The immediate context provides the interpretational insight we need.

Just prior to these statements about one's relationship with his family, Jesus had been preparing His disciples for future persecution (Matt 10:16-24). Jesus was maligned and treated poorly, so His servants cannot expect any better treatment (Matt 10:25). In order to help them persevere through such trials, Jesus mingles warning with encouragement. First, don't fear your persecutors because there is coming a day when the reality of your faith will be revealed for all to see (Matt 10:26-27). Besides, you shouldn't be afraid of those who can only kill the body, "Rather," Jesus exhorts His followers, "fear him who can destroy both soul and body in hell" (Matt 10:28). In other words, it is infinitely better to be right with God who has the power to execute eternal judgment than to escape persecution from men who only possess the power of a temporal penalty.

Furthermore, you can have confidence that your Father in heaven cares deeply for your eternal welfare. God notices when even a little sparrow falls to the ground. For this reason, you can know that God cares for those whose worth is far more than little birds (Matt 10:29-31). Professing disciples, therefore, must keep these warnings and encouragements in mind as they encounter persecution so that they will not wither in the face of opposition and deny Christ. To consistently fold in the face of persecution and deny Christ is a sign that you don't truly know Christ and will lead to Christ denying you at the final judgment (Matt 10:32-33). Those who walk in faithfulness, even amidst persecution, will receive Christ's hearty acknowledgment before His Father in heaven.

This context helps us to better understand what Jesus means in Matt 10:34-39. The issue in this passage is persecution. Jesus' coming creates division among family members because He demands ultimate loyalty. In many families those who come to Christ will be surrounded by unbelieving family members, so Jesus is preparing His disciples to be ready to endure discord where there used to be peace. When such division occurs, a professing disciple might be tempted to soften his commitment to Jesus. Such compromise is not an option, however, for Jesus calls His disciples to love Him supremely, even more than a disciple's closest relations. Those who consistently choose loyalty to family members over Jesus will find that they were never worthy of Jesus and that, while they may have gained familial peace, they lost their eternal soul (Matt 10:37-39). Those who are willing to lose even those earthly relationships that are most precious for the sake of Jesus and His gospel will find eternal life.

To love Jesus more than father and mother, therefore, means that the disciple is willing, at the moment of decision, to choose obedience to Christ over loyalty to family members, whatever the circumstance. Now that the Savior has come into the world, family is the place where true faith is either forged or surrendered.

What does this have to do with manhood? Everything. Although adult children are called to honor their parents, they are called to give Jesus Christ ultimate loyalty. A disciple of Christ now fulfills earthly obligations *out of* obedience to Christ, not *in place of* obedience to Christ. When the instructions and opinions of parents collide with the commands and wisdom of Jesus, loyalty to Jesus always prevails in the true disciple, even if that loyalty causes separation and conflict among family members.

It's important to remember, however, that when Jesus said He came to set family members against each other, it is likely that He meant that the unbeliever is the one who would be against the believer, not the other way around. Disciples of Christ are those who are meek, gentle, humble, kind, and merciful. It is unlikely that loyalty to Jesus would put a disciple "against" other people in terms of outward animosity. Paul says, "if possible, so far as it depends on you, be at peace with all men" (Rom 12:18; cf. James 3:13-18).

We must also note that Jesus said that *He* would set a man against his family members. We do not do it; Jesus does it. The presence of Jesus in the life of His disciple is what will set the unbeliever against his believing family member. The disciple, however, will be ultimately loyal to Christ, not to the family member: "Whoever loves father or mother more than me is not worthy of me, and whoever loves son or daughter more than me is not worthy of me" (Matt 10:37). We love our family members. But our love for Christ must be far greater than our love for our family members or we are not worthy of Christ.

Practically, this means that if you are living under parent's roof and they instruct you in things that are contrary to the Word of Christ in the Bible, you must obey Christ over your parents. Obedience to Christ does not mean that you are disrespectful to your parents, or harsh in your words, or looking for a fight with them. But it does mean that you will obey and follow Christ, even if following Christ comes into conflict with your parent's expectations, opinions, and counsel. "We must obey God rather than men" (Acts 5:29).

Nevertheless, you are still called to *honor* your parents (see Ex 20:12; Deut 5:16; Matt 15:1-7) so young men still living at home should honor their parents by patiently serving them, working hard to take care of the home, blessing them with thoughtful gifts, spending time with them and talking with them, and asking for forgiveness when they sin against their parents. You do not compromise on the truth in your discussions, but you also don't go looking to stir up theological controversy at every turn (see Prov 15:23; 15:28; 25:15). Loyalty to Jesus is not angry and obnoxious toward others. It is steadfast, unwavering, gentle, patient, kind, and decisive.

Also, for the sake of obedience to Christ, it is best to become financially independent from your parents as soon as you are able. This will allow you to more easily break off from your parents' control and expectations when it comes into conflict with the Word of Jesus, especially as it impacts your future plans.

The Example of Jesus Leaving Father and Mother

Leaving one's father and mother is not a mere pragmatic decision that one makes in order to prepare for marriage. As we've seen, leaving father and mother is basic to our design as men and a matter of obedience to Jesus Christ. If we are truly going to be the men God commands us to be—if we are going to fulfill the character and calling of mature manhood—then we must leave father and mother.

We see the necessity of leaving father and mother for the sake of our obedience to God most vividly in the life of Jesus Himself. Consider for a moment if Jesus had yielded to His mother's desires for His life. Despite her godliness, it is unlikely that Mary would have gladly endorsed Jesus' plan to walk into a public execution. Not even Peter, one of Jesus' closest disciples, was able to fathom such an idea (see Matt 16:22). Even during His earthly life and ministry it appears that Jesus' mother wasn't able to accurately interpret all of His actions (see Mark 3:21; Luke 2:41-51) or fully comprehend His mission (John 2:4).[2] In order to fulfill the task with which His Father entrusted Him, Jesus' love for His heavenly Father had to surpass His love for His mother. Jesus had to decisively leave His father and mother so that He could complete the mission His heavenly Father had given Him.

Mary could have interpreted this act of decisive leaving and Jesus' plan to give Himself over to an unjust execution, not as an act of love, but as an act of hatred. "How can you claim to love me and still leave me while intentionally yielding to an unjust execution without even a hint of legal recourse? You are abandoning me!" If Joseph had already died by the time Jesus began His earthly ministry, the potential pain of abandonment would have been acute.

As it turns out, Jesus' departure from His parents and His death on the cross were the most loving acts Jesus could have accomplished for His mother. What appears to be hatred for one's mother (see Luke 14:26) was actually love in its purest form (John 15:13). Yet, even though Jesus was committed to obedience to His Father and therefore maintained a course that required Him to leave His mother, He never neglected His earthly obligation to honor her. Even as Jesus is dying upon the cross, He makes sure that His mother—now without the provision and care of an eldest son—will be cared for by another capable man. "When Jesus saw his mother and the disciple whom he loved standing nearby, he said to his mother, 'Woman, behold your son!' Then he said to the disciple, 'Behold your mother!' And from that hour the disciple took her to his own home" (John 19:26-27). In Jesus we behold the perfect symmetry of love for God and love for one's neighbor, each kept in their right order and proportion. Jesus fulfills His earthly obligations, not in place of obedience to His Father, but because of it.

Should All Men Leave Father and Mother?
The growing trend in America of men remaining at home under the care, supervision, and provision of their parents is not a trend that Christian men can join or endorse. The Scriptures are clear: a man shall leave his father and mother. Leaving one's father and mother not only prepares a man for marriage; it is essential for full obedience to Jesus Christ.

But there may be times where it is appropriate for a man to remain home with his parents. One situation in which it would seem legitimate for a man to remain at home is to care for sick and dying parents. The Christian life is, fundamentally, a life of sacrifice and self-denial. It may be that you must, out of obedience to Christ, set-aside your dreams of marriage and family for a season while you care for your ailing parents. But these circumstances cannot be used as an excuse to remain fastened to one's parents for the sake of safety or provision.

A man may also need to remain at home with his parents permanently because of severe physical or mental handicaps. None of what has been said in this chapter is meant to imply that those with significant physical or mental handicaps are expected to leave father and mother in the same way that a man without these limitations is expected to leave father and mother. For some men, obedience to Christ and the fulfillment of their manhood may take shape in smaller, yet just as significant ways while they remain dependent upon their parents for care and provision.

For most men, however, the call is to leave father and mother. And we must be wary of legitimate *sounding* reasons for why we have yet to fulfill this call on our lives. Financial concerns often carry significant weight in a man's decision to remain within the comfortable confines of his parents' home. Rent-free or close-to-rent-free living certainly helps pad the savings account, but it robs a man of something far more valuable: character forged by sacrifice, deferred desires, simplicity, and the God-ordained satisfaction of providing for oneself. And we've already touched on this above, but a man who has left his parent's financial oversight may still be unwilling to leave the comfort of his parent's spiritual and emotional guidance. We must ask the Lord to search our hearts and reveal where we might be hiding fear and cowardice behind a guise of what we've come to call "wisdom" or "preparing for the future."

Conclusion

Becoming the men God has called us to be requires that we leave father and mother. We may be faithful to church, regular in Bible reading and prayer, and committed to discipleship, but if we are not willing to leave father and mother, we will never grow into the men we were made to be. Unfortunately, we live in a culture that is less and less likely to uphold this requirement for men. It is far more acceptable now for men to remain at home with their parents into their late-twenties than it was even twenty years ago.

The call of Genesis 2:24, therefore, may be unsettling, even offensive, for some Christian men. At least, it won't seem very compelling in light of what the culture currently values and respects. To boldly take upon oneself the responsibilities of manhood in one's late teens and early twenties will appear more and more out-of-step with societal expectations. But when has Christianity ever been fully validated by the surrounding culture? The call to biblical manhood, though a glorious, fulfilling, dignified calling, will be, at best, ignored by the present culture; despised at worst. But let's not allow these contrary currents to discourage us from making headway on our course to true manhood. Courage, as we've already noted, is a necessary component of biblical manhood, and perseverance, too. And we will need both as we leave father and mother.

7

Singleness and Mature Manhood

Throughout this book it has been my goal to help us better understand what God requires of men and how we might grow, by God's grace, into the men we have been created and re-created to be. A few questions remain unanswered, however. The first set of questions relates to single men. The second set relates to the resources we need to grow in mature manhood. I will address the first set of questions in this chapter, and the second set of questions in chapter eight.

Singleness and Mature Manhood

I began this book by taking us through Genesis 2-3. By starting in Genesis, it was inevitable that I would frame much of our discussion on manhood with reference to marriage. There is nothing wrong with this approach, for it is Scripture itself that defines manhood, by and large, with reference to marriage. Nevertheless, I have sought throughout this book to speak directly to the single man in order to help him apply the truth of Scripture to his own situation. It is my hope that these sections have been helpful and clarifying for you, and that you do not feel as though you are left out of the discussion due to your marital status.

I believe there are good, biblical reasons why a man may be single. Paul himself commends singleness for its many advantages and indicates that singleness enables one to cultivate a life of undivided spiritual focus. A man *does not* need a wife in order to fulfill his Christian calling.[1] But we must have the spiritual wherewithal to be honest with our motives and determine if fear is actually keeping us from pursuing something good, like marriage.

For example, you might recognize that the calling to provide for a wife and children is a high and potentially difficult calling. You know that it will require sacrifice, hard work, and self-denial, and you may be intimidated at the prospect of having a woman and small children depend fully on you for their shelter and physical sustenance. If you are intimidated at the thought of providing for a family, it might be because you rightly understand what is at stake and how serious this responsibility really is. That's good. I am glad you appreciate the gravity of this high calling.

But if you wallow in fear and allow it to drive you *from* marriage rather than *to* God, then you are in danger of compromising your manhood. I am not saying that all men must be married. It may be that God has called you to a life of singleness so that you might serve Him with a singularity of focus. But this calling is not for all men, and it is probably not for most. When Paul broached the topic of singleness in his first letter to the Corinthian church, he did so by first acknowledging that marriage is the normal state for adults and will be the calling of most people (1 Cor 7:1-5). Singleness has significant advantages when it comes to ministry and service (1 Cor 7:32-35), but such a calling will not be for everyone (1 Cor 7:6-7).

Paul even helps us discern whether or not we have the gift

of singleness when he says, referring to unmarried Christians, "But if they cannot exercise self-control, they should marry. For it is better to marry than to burn with passion" (1 Cor 7:9). The primary indicator of whether a man possesses the gift of singleness is located in his desires. Do you have a strong and consistent desire to marry and fulfill your sexual desires? If so, then it is unlikely that you have the gift of singleness.

But the current rise in average age among Christian men getting married, is not due, in most cases, to their decision to devote themselves wholly to ministry. There are other factors, many related to fear of commitment, the myth of compatibility, fear of assuming greater responsibility, illegitimate financial concerns, the desire to remain in perpetual freedom, fear of rejection, and pornography. Let's discuss each of these.

Fear of Commitment

"The exclusiveness of marriage," one author has eloquently noted, "is the essence of marriage."[2] Marriage, by its very nature, is an exclusive commitment to another person of undivided affection and sexual fidelity for the rest of one's life. When we say "I do," we are, among other things, "forsaking all others."[3] Once you are married, you have closed the door to all other options. The woman to whom you just recited your vows is the one for you, "until death do you part."

The prospect of finally saying "this is the one" can provoke fear and reluctance in some single men. Will I regret my choice? What if someone better comes along? Questions like these can unsettle a man and tempt him to remain in a state of perpetual dating or withdraw from pursuing a relationship altogether. But such fear certainly is not the mark of mature manhood, nor should it be entertained as a legitimate reason for remaining unmarried.

Such fear is usually rooted in pride. When a man thinks highly of himself—of his physical appearance, his talents, his maturity, his accomplishments—he will find it difficult to commit to a woman. Thoughts of finding someone better only fill the mind of the man who thinks he is worthy of the perfect girl.

Pride also keeps us from rightly beholding the beauty of the women around us. Physical attraction is important, but it cannot be ultimate when considering a potential wife. The most physically attractive woman in the world who despises the Lord will, over time, become repulsive in the eyes of a godly man (see Prov 11:22). Likewise, a woman's godliness will accentuate her physical beauty, and will, over time, become the most precious feature of her personhood to a man walking in biblical manhood (see Prov 31:30). Pride and a sense of self-importance, however, will blind us from what is most valuable. But if we begin with the soul-cleansing truth that we—all of us—deserve hell, much less a wife, we will be far more likely to commit to one woman. Once we've seen what we really deserve, that simple, godly Christian girl we've been dating for eighteen months begins to look very attractive, almost irresistible.

None of this is meant to suggest that a single Christian man should toss biblical expectations for a spouse to the wind and marry the next woman who comes along. If you are a Christian, you can only marry another Christian (1 Cor 7:39; cf. 2 Cor 6:14). And there is wisdom in pursuing a woman who exemplifies some basic, though not perfect, elements of Christian character, as we just noted. The point is simply this:

make sure that you are not delaying marriage because you think you are God's gift to women. That is a mark of tremendous immaturity, not maturity.

Believing the Myth of "Compatibility"

Another hindrance to marriage could be a man's wrong thinking about so-called compatibility. It seems that much is often made of compatibility when it comes to considering whom one should pursue and marry. But the idea of compatibility is not biblical, nor is it helpful. As one biblical counselor explains,

> Ordinarily when one uses the word [compatibility] in modern speech he means that two persons have personalities, interests, and backgrounds that are compatible and that, therefore, they would be more likely to make a good marriage than if these elements in each were diverse. There is no evidence in Scripture that this is true. To think that because socio-economic levels are similar or because both persons like tennis or because both fathers wear gray-flannel suits to work, these factors will give a young couple the edge in marriage is an idea without Biblical foundation.[4]

Despite the popular notion that single men and women should strive to find someone with whom they are "compatible," this author rightly argues that "The Biblical fact is that no two persons are compatible, regardless of whether their backgrounds [are] similar or not."[5] Why does he dismiss wholesale the concept of compatibility? Because "we are all born sinners, and that means that we are by nature incompatible people."[6] The truth is that a couple could have many things in common but still endure significant conflict because they are proud and selfish.[7] Relational trouble occurs when our desires overtake our love for one another, not because he likes movies and she likes the outdoors (see James 4:1-2).

Biblically, there are only three factors for men to consider when thinking about compatibility. First, there is sexual compatibility. Is the person in whom you are interested a women? If so, then by nature you are compatible (Gen 2:24-25). Second is spiritual compatibility. Is the person with whom you are interested a genuine Christian? If so, then you are spiritually compatible (see 1 Cor 7:39; cf. 2 Cor 6:14-15). Third, there is gender-roles compatibility.

Because of the influence of feminism in the evangelical Church over the past four decades, it is no longer assured that a Christian man and woman will be in agreement over gender roles. But because gender roles comprise the very essence of a man and women's relationship in marriage, how you each understand these roles will have a deep and lasting effect on your life as a married couple. If you believe what I have developed in this book with regard to men and women's roles is the teaching of Scripture, but your girlfriend or fiancé doesn't, the question you must ask is, Who is going to compromise? Which one of you will choose to violate your conscience in order to have "peace" in the home?[8] My point in asking these questions is not to encourage compromise on this vital issue, but to highlight that a man and woman must make sure they are in agreement at this point of gender roles, or they are setting themselves up for significant spiritual and relational trouble.

When it comes to compatibility, only these three items should be considered. When you add other items alongside these three factors for the compatibility of your future spouse, you are keeping yourself from the blessing of marriage.

Fear of Greater Responsibility

The responsibility to provide for a wife and children is a weighty burden. Your new wife and, someday, your children, will look to you to work hard, earn a steady income, and provide for their material needs. If your finances start to become a little shaky, if the economy plummets, if home prices sky-rocket, the responsibility is on you as the man to do whatever it takes, within legitimate means, to care for your family.

And with added family members comes additional constraints upon your time. Your new wife will desire time together, and, when children come along, so will they. You will be responsible to lead your family spiritually, to consistently teach your children biblical truth, and to sacrifice time to participate in the activities that interest them. As a husband and father, you will need to care for your home or apartment, oversee the finances, protect your family members from spiritual and physical harm, set the spiritual tone for your family, and bear the weight of difficult decision-making.

All of these duties will require you to sacrifice several of the things you enjoy doing. You will have to give up many of your hobbies and interests and finally say goodbye to many of your frivolous pursuits. Video games, binge-watching movies and television, aimless surfing of the Internet, religious devotion to sports and sports teams, excessive exercise, and other similar activities will need to be set-aside for the good of your family.

Desire for Perpetual Freedom

Related to the fear of greater responsibility is the desire for perpetual freedom. After many years of discipling young men, reading books on the subject of manhood, and reflecting on pertinent sociological studies, it has become clear to me that one of the primary reasons why men in America are waiting longer and longer to get married is because they simply want to maintain their freedom.

Young men are experiencing life in an economic context of unparalleled affluence, which affords them not only a job and a place to live, but a wealth of opportunity for adventure, travel, recreation, social engagement, and, well, just doing whatever they want to do. Simply put: due to our financial resources, technology, and the general shift over the past century from an agricultural-industrial society to an information-based society, we have access to more time and money than ever before in human history.

Marriage, however, limits this freedom. We now must give ourselves constantly to another rather than just to ourselves. Our time, energy, and resources must now be channeled in the direction of our wife and children, and our decisions must be made in reference to them. The "peace" we once enjoyed is now interrupted by the needs of a wife and family. But this peace that we treasured may not have been the peace of Christ. As one author explains,

> A certain kind of manufactured calm can come to those who don't wish to be parents or who abandon their children to the welfare state or to the abortionist's sword. This kind of freedom doesn't startle you out of a midnight slumber or cause you to run your anxious hands through your

hair in frustration. No one is watching to see how you trained up a new generation to worship or spurn the God of your fathers.

But what an impoverished sense of pseudo-*Shalom* this must be. It's the peace of a beggar who is content to glean from the fields while never risking the possibility of failing as a farmer. There's a high price to pay for such peace.[9]

A high price, indeed. While we think we have really hit the sweet spot of male existence by remaining in the bliss of unencumbered freedom, we are actually militating against our manhood, and, ironically, robbing ourselves of true happiness. "It is more blessed to give than receive," Jesus said during His earthly ministry (see Acts 20:35), and when we sacrifice our so-called freedom in order to accept the burden of greater responsibility, we will find, among the toil and anxiety, a deep and satisfying joy.

Illegitimate Financial Concerns

Another reason why men are delaying marriage is because they believe they are unable to provide for a wife and children. And, in their present state, it may be true that they are unable to, based on their current income, support a wife and children. That's why they are currently living in their parent's basement. But we have to ask what these young men really believe about "provision." If they think they need to provide a large home, in-ground swimming pool, two luxury vehicles, and quarterly vacations to international destinations, then they will become convinced that pursuing marriage can only happen well into their late-twenties or early thirties, if at all.

But we have to be careful that we don't replace the biblical requirement for provision with an ideal formed by the historically unprecedented affluence of the United States. Food, clothing, and a place to live are all that a family needs. And if a man can provide those things, he is eligible for marriage. I do not mean to suggest that a young man should use these minimal requirements as an excuse for laziness and perpetually hanging by a financial thread. As we've noted throughout this book already, a strong work ethic is essential to mature manhood, and a man should find ways to bless his family, not merely provide for their most basic needs. But delaying marriage in order to stockpile enough cash to supply your future wife with a three-car garage and regular trips to the Virgin Islands is wholly unnecessary.

This discussion is also important for dads with daughters old enough to be married. Fathers are right to be concerned over their daughter's future provision under the care of another man. This concern is normal and good. But when a dad begins to attach non-biblical requirements to his list of qualifications for his daughter's suitors, he is in danger of acting contrary to God's design and training his daughter to value the wrong things.

Dads, if you are holding your daughter's boyfriend to a biblical standard, you will be primarily concerned about his personal holiness, integrity, love for Jesus, faithfulness to the local church, and his work ethic. To bump him off the list of possible husbands either directly to his face or indirectly by undermining his character to your daughter because he does not fit a specific financial profile—beyond the basic requirements of an ability to provide food, clothing, and shelter—you are teaching your daughter to become a lover of money, and this will prove deadly to her soul (see Matt 6:19-

34; Luke 12:13-34). If a young man is walking with Jesus, expressing Christian maturity, and able to provide your daughter with the basics of life, he is eligible to marry her, whether he has an E-Trade account or not.

Fear of Rejection

Another reason why some men remain single is because they fear rejection. To initiate conversation and finally ask a woman out to coffee or dinner takes a little courage, and some men simply lack the nerve to risk a woman's negative response. Due to some social awkwardness or past rejections, some men simply forego the blessing of marriage because they are unwilling to take the first step. Given the direct connection we find in Scripture between courage and manhood, we can say with confidence that fear of rejection is an illegitimate reason for remaining single. If your fear of rejection is keeping you from pursuing a woman, the answer for you is to ask God for help, be "strong and courageous," and do something about it.

But if you have faced rejection once, twice, or on several occasions, perhaps it is time to consider why you are not finding success. As a wise friend of mine once said, "Some people are single for a season. Some people are single for a reason."[10] Are you single for a reason? Could you be at fault for singleness because you simply don't attend to your physical appearance and hygiene? Do you take care of yourself by exercising and eating well? Do you dress in a way that is dignified and expresses intentionality and maturity? Do you shower, comb your hair, and brush your teeth on a regular basis? I am not asking if you are aware of the latest clothing trends or if your body resembles the guys on the cover of Men's Fitness. What I am asking is if you are pursuing an "un-distracting attractiveness"[11] in how you care for your physical appearance. A Christian who is growing in mature manhood will not worship his physical appearance, but he will not neglect it either.

But it is also important to ask if you are regularly facing rejection because you have never learned to talk to a woman. What I am referring to here is the ability to engage a woman in conversation by talking about her life and interests, discussing important topics related to Christ, Scripture, the Church, your local community, and the world, and actively listening to what she says. It is far too easy for us guys to become engrossed in our own interests and achievements that we either dominate the conversation with stories about ourselves, or we withdraw and wait for the woman to ask us questions. But if God has created us to lead, then we must lead in our conversations with women. And if God has called us to love, then we must love our sisters in Christ by actively listening to them and taking an interest in what they say.

Addiction to Pornography

Finally, we come to the tough but necessary issue of pornography. The use of pornography among men, including professing Christian men, is significant. Consider these statistics. According to a study conducted in 2014 by the Barna Group, 79% of 18-30 year-olds surveyed admitted to viewing pornography at least once a month, while 67% of 31-49-year-olds and 49% of 50-68-year-olds confessed to this same frequency of use. Perhaps most alarming is the fact that among those surveyed, 63% of 18-30-year-olds, 38% of 31-49-year-olds, and 25% of 50-68-year-olds stated that they view pornography multiple times a week. Overall, 55% of married men and 70% of unmarried men confess to using pornography once a month.[12] These stats should stagger us.

I have often wondered if the growing use of pornography among men in America is one reason—perhaps one of the primary reasons—why men are waiting longer and longer to get married. The apostle Peter tells us that fleshly lusts are not something with which to trifle, because they "wage war against your soul" (1 Peter 2:11). Because pornography is a perversion of God's good gift of human sexuality, it distorts the minds of its users toward this good gift and disables people from using it appropriately.

Pornography promotes relational selfishness and creates unrealistic, unhealthy expectations for sexual intimacy while greatly weakening a man's ability to delight in his wife's physical beauty. Through constant pornography use, young men have lost their ability to appreciate the beauty and goodness of the women around them and have become satisfied with a digital harem who will not only do all their bidding, but who will not bother him with difficulties that attend real relationships.

As a result, men are reluctant to engage—and in some severe cases, incapacitated from engaging—women in genuine relationship and commitment. My encouragement to you is that you would consider how pornography has played or is presently playing a role in your singleness. You may not think pornography has kept you from marriage, but I can assure you, if you are currently looking at pornography on a regular basis or if you have indulged in pornography in the past, it most certainly has served to keep you from marriage, whether you are perceptible of its negative effects or not.

You must also be aware of how pornography use decreases your desires for marriage. I noted above that a lack of a strong and consistent desire for marriage and sexual fulfillment is a sign that you might have the gift of singleness. But you must be careful that you don't mistake lack of desire due to frequent pornography use as a God-given gift of singleness. If you think you have the gift of singleness because you don't consider your desire for marriage to be particularly acute, yet you are engaging in pornography and masturbation on a regular basis, you have deceived yourself about your current state. The reason you don't have a compelling desire to be married is because you are presently fulfilling your sexual desires through pornography. This is *not* the gift of singleness. A man can only be confident that he has the gift of singleness if he is lacks a strong desire for sexual fulfillment *and* he is able to keep himself sexually pure.

If you are currently enmeshed in pornography, it is time to repent. Confess your sin, not only to God, but also to a trusted, more mature brother in Christ who will help you climb out of the mire of sexual sin. It is unlikely that you will find your way out of your singleness until you find your way out of pornography.

Conclusion

Again, it bears repeating: none of what I have said in this chapter is meant to suggest that single Christian men are second-class Christians or that you are unable to fulfill your Christian calling without being married. Jesus and Paul dignified singleness and showed us that one needs not be married to be fully human or to fulfill God's calling on one's life. Nor do I mean to suggest that the reason you are not currently married *must* be one of the aforementioned reasons. There are godly, single Christian men who are bearing the weight of significant responsibility, diligently serving others, exhibiting maturity, and walking in sexual purity. I praise God for these men, and I admire their commitment to Christ.

Nevertheless, it is also the case that many single Christian men are avoiding marriage, not for admirable reasons, but for self-centered ones. My aim in this chapter was to help you think through the issue of manhood as it relates to singleness and marriage in order to determine if you are delaying marriage due to pride, selfishness, or wrong thinking about who you are in Christ. Ask the Lord to search your heart and life and reveal if any of these things might be true of you (Ps 139:23-24). As the Lord exposes your heart, you may begin to feel as though the weight of mature manhood is impossible to bear. Don't worry. It *is* impossible to bear. But Christ has given you every resource you need to carry out this calling. Whether we are single or married, we have all that we need in order to fulfill our manhood. As we make use of these resources, we will find that Jesus' yoke is easy, and His burden, light (Matt 11:30). We turn now to discuss these resources in chapter eight.

8

The Resources You Need (And Have in Christ!)

Unless you've been merely skimming these past seven chapters, it is likely that you are beginning to feel the weight of manhood growing heavier upon your shoulders. Yes, there is excitement to become the man God has created and re-created you to be. But there is also intimidation, uncertainty, and a sense of inadequacy. That's fine. These feelings just mean that you recognize the seriousness of what God calls you to as a man.

But Christianity is not merely about obeying commandments to "be a man" or to "do hard things." Yes, we must be men (1 Cor 16:13) and face difficulty with courage. But when confronted with significant challenges to our manhood, it doesn't take supernatural grace to muster up enough will power to muscle our way through some duties and add some hard work and resolve to our daily routine. But these attempts at change and growth will be short-lived, and they will typically be characterized by frustration, inconsistency, and a palpable lack of kindness toward loved ones.

No, unlike every other religion in the world, Christianity begins, ends, and is sustained at every point by the grace of

Christ apart from our works (Rom 3:27). Grace, not mature manhood, sets us right with God. And grace, not growth in mature manhood, keeps us right with God. In order to become the men God has called us to be, we must first stop attempting to get right with God by becoming the men God has called us to be.

Start Here: The Gospel and Justification

The first resource with which God has supplied us to grow into mature men is the good news of Jesus Christ. Our immaturity, cowardice, and passivity are problems. But they are not our biggest problem. At the root of all of these issues is sin. We are sinful by nature and by choice, and we stand, therefore, condemned before God. We have broken the entirety of God's law, for when we are guilty of one commandment, we rend the whole piece (James 2:10). Our state is so desperate, the Scripture tells us that we don't even have the inclination to seek for God (Rom 3:10-12), for we are dead in our sins (Eph 2:1-3) and set against God from the core of who we are. In our natural state, all we do is sin (Rom 8:7).

In light of our desperate situation, we might attempt to obey the laws we have broken, like a child attempting to appease his father by putting the shattered window back together piece by piece. But this cannot work, for it is impossible for sinners to be declared righteous by keeping the law (Rom 3:19-20). Why? Because our obedience cannot atone for our sin, and our attempts at keeping the law just reveal the depth of our depravity (Rom 7:8-13). We may not commit adultery, but our heart lusts after other women (Matt 5:28). We may not steal from others, but we covet what we don't have and serve the idols of greed in our own hearts (Col

130

3:5). Indeed, the more we attempt to obey the law for our right standing before God, the more we grow to hate it.

The pursuit of mature manhood, therefore, cannot begin until this precarious situation is remedied. We need to be delivered from our condemnation, not by our works, but apart from our works, in order to walk in newness of life and godly maturity. This is precisely what God provides for us in the gospel. God sent His Son, Jesus Christ, God of very God, fully equal to His Father in every way, to become a man, to live a life of perfect righteousness in our place and to pay the penalty of death in our place. Where Adam was *passive* and disobedient to God's commandments, Jesus *actively* fulfilled all of God's commandments in our place (Matt 3:15) and, *actively* died on the cross in our place (John 10:18), paying the penalty for all of our disobedience. After Christ paid for our sins by His death, He rose from the dead and ascended to heaven to intercede before God for His people.

It was God's plan to accomplish our salvation entirely apart from us and outside of us in order that He would receive all the glory and we would receive all the joy. By faith in Christ alone we receive God's gift of justification, which is nothing less than God's declaration of our right standing with Him on the basis of Jesus Christ alone. Even at the moment of our justification we are still ungodly: "And to the one who does not work but believes in him who justifies the ungodly, his faith is counted as righteousness (Rom 4:5). This declaration of righteousness is unchanging and provides us with full access to God through Christ. We have peace with our Father and will never again face His wrath.

The moment we are justified, we begin a new life. God's Spirit has come to indwell our hearts, and we have, by the new birth, received new spiritual affections. We have a new love for God and for others. We desire to keep God's Word, not in order to be right with Him, but because we already are, and because we now love that law (Ps 119:97; Jer 31:33). A true pursuit of mature manhood, therefore, is conducted from a heart that is free from the need to secure our salvation by our mature manhood.

It is vital that we are solid on these gospel truths. Unless we are certain that our right relationship with God is not, in any way, dependent upon our growth in godly masculinity, we will become easily discouraged, frustrated, and either rush headlong into male domination or retreat into cowardly passivity. But when the gospel is clear in the eyes of our heart and mind, we will find that our growth will be steady, and our relationships with others will be approached from a posture of humility and gentleness.

Remain Here: The Gospel and the Local Church

No matter how sound your doctrine of salvation is, however, you will upend your pursuit of mature masculinity if you attempt a lone venture. By God's design the gospel brings us into fellowship with other believers for the sake of our growth and perseverance in the faith. So vital is a believer's connection to other believers that Paul likens the Church to a body. We rightly consider it gruesome and out of place when body parts are detached from the body to which they belong. What was once normal, even beautiful, is now grotesque because it is isolated from the body (see 1 Cor 12:12-25). When CNN reports that five severed feet have washed up on the shores of British Columbia, no one wonders why such reports are newsworthy.[1] Feet are usually nothing to get excited about. But feet detached from bodies and floating in the ocean? That's a problem.

It is no wonder, therefore, why Paul uses the body as an apt illustration of how Christ has composed His Church. When a member is severed from the rest of the body—that is, cut off from regular fellowship with believers, corporate worship, and the accountability of the local church and its leaders—not only is that church affected, but that person begins to look unnatural and out of place. Often, when Christians remove themselves from the regular fellowship and accountability of the local church, pride begins to fester, sin takes deeper root, and strange beliefs tend to wedge their way into the wandering Christian's heart and mind. I've seen it happen many, many times.

Conversely, when we remain vitally connected to the local church through regular corporate worship, hearing the Word, accountability, fellowship, and faithful service, we will gird ourselves with the God-ordained means for spiritual stability and growth. Let's consider each of these aspects of local church life.

Worship

While it is true that our whole lives as Christians are an act of worship (see Rom 12:1-2), it is also true that corporate worship is a time of unique blessing. God has composed a *people*, not just individuals, and He delights in hearing a chorus of believing men and women, boys and girls, exalting His name and praising His Son through singing, public reading of Scripture, preaching, and giving. Corporate worship not only glorifies God, it offers a unique blessing to believers as well. We enjoy God and Christ through heart-felt singing, and we are encouraged in our faith as we hear the collective praise of our brothers and sisters in Christ. Such worship strengthens our hearts and deepens our love for God and other believers.

These regular times of corporate worship are vital to keep our relationship with the Lord grounded in a right heart posture. Ultimately, our pursuit of mature manhood must be motivated by a love for God and a love for people, and these affections are kindled and sustained by regular corporate worship.

Hearing the Word

But worship doesn't consist only of singing praise *to* the living God; it also includes hearing *from* the living God. Preaching has always been the centerpiece of true corporate worship, ever since the days of Israel through the early New Testament Church. And it was during the Reformation in the 1500s that biblical preaching was recaptured in a significant sense as the centerpiece of public worship.[2] The Reformers understood that the preaching of Scripture is the primary means by which God speaks to and communicates His presence to His people. We are instructed, rebuked, corrected, encouraged, convicted, renewed, endowed with faith, and spurred to obedience through the preaching of God's Word. Personal Bible reading and study are both important for our spiritual growth, but these disciplines should never be sought *in place of* regular hearing of the Word, but pursued alongside it. And we never progress in godly manhood unless we regularly place ourselves under the preaching of God's Word.

Accountability

Alongside of regular worship and hearing the Word preached, we need the local church body for accountability. Such accountability is not optional. In fact, God has ordained accountability to be a means by which we persevere in the faith. If we have believed in Christ with saving faith, we cannot be lost (see John 10:27-30; Rom 8:31-39). But God has established means by which He keeps us believing in Christ. One of those means is hearing the Word (Rom 10:17), as we noted above. Another is accountability. Listen to these words from the book of Hebrews.

> Take care, brothers, lest there be in any of you an evil, unbelieving heart, leading you to fall away from the living God. But exhort one another every day, as long as it is called "today," that none of you may be hardened by the deceitfulness of sin. For we have come to share in Christ, if indeed we hold our original confidence firm to the end (Heb 3:12-14).

This passage makes it clear that it is the responsibility of believers to watch out for their fellow brothers and sisters. The book of Hebrews answers Cain's infamous question from centuries ago, "Am I my brother's keeper" (Gen 4:9) with a resounding "Yes!" By regularly exhorting each other with biblical warnings and inducements, we are to make sure that none of the professing believers in our local church are "hardened by the deceitfulness of sin." The Church, therefore, is the place where we are kept spiritually safe and guarded from apostasy. Mutual admonishment and encouragement is not optional. It is God's design that we persevere in the faith by the means of our brothers' and sisters' exhortations. Note verse 14: "For we have come to share in Christ, if indeed we hold our original confidence firm to the end."

The only way we can have assurance that we have come to "share in Christ" is if "we hold our original confidence firm to the end," and the warnings and encouragements of our brothers and sisters are the means by which we are able to hold our confidence firm to the end. The author of Hebrews is not suggesting that true believers can lose their salvation; he is confident that his listeners will not fall away from Christ (see Heb 10:39). Nevertheless, he also recognizes that God works through means, and the means by which He keeps His people in the faith is by placing them in the church where they will regularly hear the exhortations of faithful brothers and sisters.

It should be obvious, therefore, when thinking about biblical manhood why accountability is so important. The health, vitality, and, ultimately, the perseverance of our spiritual lives depend on it. Men, it is not enough to walk in and out of church every Sunday. We need friendships with brothers who will ask us the tough questions, tell us what we need to hear even when we don't want to hear it, and call us back to faithfulness when we are drifting (James 5:19-20). We must be willing to open ourselves up to the tough love of older, wiser brothers who have the courage to speak the truth in love. And we must be willing to be honest with our sins and struggles. Without the accountability of close gospel relationships, our progress in godly masculinity will stall and sputter, and, potentially, come to nothing.

Fellowship
We also need to rub shoulders with other brothers in a variety of settings and circumstances. Yes, we need the times of serious discussion and accountability. But we also need to simply share life with our church family so that we can watch and learn from our brothers as they interact with others, raise their families, deal with difficulty, persevere through trials, and repent from sin. We need to be with other Christian men at the ballpark and at the funeral home; at the Christmas

concert and at the hospital; sharing a meal or watching a movie. Disciples learn from verbal instruction, but they also learn by observation and nearness to other godly men (see Mark 3:14).

Personally, I cannot say enough about the sanctifying power and spiritual effectiveness of the local church in my life as a man. God has used relationships with other godly men—those older *and* younger than me—to be a vital means of instruction, warning, encouragement, rebuke, and admonishment. I've learned by their example, benefitted from their loving correction, gained wisdom from their counsel, and been kept from many a sin because of these friendships. In other words, God has used my brothers in the local church to help me persevere in the faith. I shudder to think where I would be if it were not for these men.

Brothers, we need these kinds of relationships if we are going to grow in mature manhood, and we will only benefit from the example and counsel of other men as we are around them. Fellowship is a vital part of church life and a necessary component in our pursuit of mature manhood.

Service

Another vital element to local church life is service. We are called to "serve one another" (Gal 5:13) out of love and a desire to bless and benefit fellow believers. It is for this reason that every Christian has been endowed with a spiritual gift (1 Cor 12:7). Service is essential to growing in mature manhood because it bends us toward ministry to others while drawing us out of ourselves. One of the distressing trends among young men in America, noted by Gary Cross in his book *Men to Boys*, is their growing obsession with and devotion to *self*. While aware of the possibility of romanticizing earlier generations, Cross notes that there was a time—reflected particularly in the "Greatest Generation"—where men more naturally walked in patterns of manhood that were others-orientated. Service to country and, afterward, giving oneself to the "self-denying settings of marriage and family"[3] was the ordinary pattern of adult manhood.

Much has changed over the past seventy years, however, and today men appear to be characterized more by a relentless pursuit of pleasure, perpetual youth, and unencumbered freedom than they are by hearty desire to selflessly serve others. But the gospel of Christ saves us from this kind of vain existence and sets us on a course to find lasting pleasure by seeking it in the happiness and benefit of others. Mature manhood can only grow deep roots in the soil of worship, solid preaching, fellowship, and accountability. But healthy manhood won't terminate on self; it will be productive for the good of others; not for the praise of man (Matt 6:1), but for the praise that comes from God (see Rom 2:29; Matt 25:21).

End (and Start Again) Here:
The Gospel and Failure

One danger in talking about biblical manhood is the possibility of unintentionally encouraging men to produce godly masculinity by the strength of their own will power. And it should be no surprise that some men's ministries have been guilty of doing exactly this. In their excitement to motivate men to fulfill their calling as leaders, protectors, and providers, some pastors and teachers have wrested the biblical command to "act like men" from the context of the gospel, consequently separating the fruit of mature manhood from the vital nutrient of God's grace.

After hearing the exhortations to mature manhood, men with naturally aggressive personalities will often charge ahead, pursuing their duties with all their might. But, because they have not been taught how the gospel provides the framework for their effort to grow as men, these men tend to be overbearing, domineering, and characterized by pride. When these men experience failure in their attempts at growth, they will often become angry and will, because of their pride, cover up their mistakes and sins. Because of their aggressive personalities, these men may not be derailed from their pursuit of mature manhood—they are the kind of guys who "get things done"—but the fruit of their efforts will be intimidating male domination, not mature manhood.

While they may not be in danger of becoming overbearing or domineering, men with more reserved personalities, when confronted with a raw, in-your-face exhortation to "grow up" and "act like men" apart from the gospel, will be cast into discouragement before they even begin their venture into mature masculinity. "If manhood is achieved by the sheer force of will," they might reason, "then surely those with CEO-type personalities will be the most successful in their pursuit of biblical manhood." Despair may characterize men who are naturally less assertive and aggressive.

The answer for these two kinds of men—and every man along this spectrum—is the good news of Jesus Christ. And the answer will always be the good news of Jesus Christ, especially when we fail in our pursuit of mature masculinity. We've already noted how important it is to place our exhortations within the context of the gospel: we are made right with God by His grace alone, through Christ alone, not by our efforts at becoming mature men. This glorious truth levels our pride and any sense that we are superior to others.

But this truth also teaches us that we are unable to make any progress in the faith apart from God's grace. Personality type, while an important factor, isn't ultimately decisive in our growth in manhood. The fruit of masculine maturity is the fruit of the Holy Spirit, not will power (see Gal 5:22-23). Our wills are involved, but only insofar as they are enabled by the Holy Spirit. We are to "labor" and "strive" and "make every effort" (1 Thess 1:3; Luke 13:24; Heb 4:11; 12:14; 2 Pet 1:5) to put off sin and grow in holiness; but we don't pursue these things in order to get God to save us or to work in us. God has already justified us by grace apart from our works, and now, because of that justification, He works in us by His Spirit to produce the fruit that is pleasing to Him. "Work out your own salvation with fear and trembling," Paul reminded the Philippians, "*for* it is God who works in you, both to will and to work for his good pleasure" (Phil 2:12-13; see also Heb 13:21). God is already at work in believers. For this reason, work out the salvation that you already possess. To reverse this process even a fraction of a degree is to undermine the entire sanctification process.

Grace, therefore, humbles the man who is tempted to lean on his will power to produce maturity, and grace encourages the man who is concerned about his growth because he isn't naturally a go-getter. And grace reminds both kinds of men that failure is something that should not be hidden—from God or from others. If we are justified wholly by the grace of Christ apart from our works, then we have no need to raise an unrealistic façade of pseudo-maturity for the sake of impressing others. God has saved us by pure grace, so we no longer have anything to boast in, including our own righteousness. We no longer need to perform righteous deeds in order to be seen by others (Matt 6:1), for we have God's eternal approval through Christ, and that is all the approval we need.

After describing in detail how God had provided, in Christ, full atonement for our sin (see Rom 3:21-26), the apostle Paul concludes, "Then what becomes of our boasting? It is excluded. By what kind of law? By a law of works? No, but by the law of faith. For we hold that one is justified by faith apart from works of the law" (Rom 3:27-28). The very design of our salvation destroys all boasting in ourselves. But when we attempt to cover up our sins and failures from God's eyes (which is impossible) and the eyes of others, we are actually indulging in a kind of boasting. Granted, it may not seem like boasting because we tend to think of boasting in more active terms. When we cover up our sin, it doesn't feel like we are boasting because we aren't actively speaking highly of ourselves or purposefully engaging in an activity in order to impress others.

But we are boasting just the same. When we refuse to confess and admit our sins and mistakes to others, we are laboring to *make it appear* as though we are more mature, more spiritually advanced, more holy, and more righteous than we really are, and this is nothing less than boasting in ourselves. But the gospel frees us from such tyranny. Because we have been saved by grace apart from any righteousness of our own and are secure eternally in Christ, we can willingly confess our sins and mistakes to both God and others. Despair need not bury us when we fail in our efforts to become the men God has called us to be. Our Father is fully satisfied in His Son, who has always been the man God called Him to be and because of our union with the Son, God is fully satisfied in us. From this spiritually comforting truth we are able to move ahead in our pursuit of mature manhood. Guilt, raw exhortation, and appeal to will power cannot produce the fruit of mature manhood. Only the grace of Jesus Christ and the Holy Spirit can do that.

Conclusion

God has not left us alone. His divine power, as Peter reminds us, has given us everything necessary for life and godliness (2 Pet 1:3). Everything necessary. He has given us His Son, His gospel, His Church, and His Spirit to enable us to walk in godly masculinity. Regardless of our background, our personality type, our marital status, or any other factor, we can begin to take strides in fulfilling our calling as men. May God be merciful to us in our pursuit of mature manhood.

Conclusion

We must admit that Gary Cross is right: there is a growing lack of male maturity in America. Men, by and large, are struggling to figure out what it means to be truly masculine, and much of this same struggle is found in the Church where guys, though committed to Jesus Christ, are left without adequate instruction and example as to what it means to be a godly, mature man. Some churches who seek to remedy this problem may, out of good intention, depict manhood in ways that appeal to men with certain personality types or interests that our society exalts as "manly," while failing to go to the root of our problem and addressing this problem with Scripture. As a result, men who do not fit the cultural mold of so-called masculinity are either disillusioned in their pursuit of manhood or estranged from those men who exhibit more aggressive personalities.

In this book I have sought to draw our attention to the biblical calling and expectation of men in order to avoid unduly emphasizing or enshrining societal marks of mature masculinity and, rather, cast a vision of manhood that all men can embrace; not because I am particularly clever, but because I have sought to ground our convictions in unchanging truth. By taking us all the way back to Genesis, I argued that our passivity is basic to our problems as guys and that our failure to actively lead has, since that fateful day in the Garden of Eden, resulted in widespread misery. Our passivity may not have introduced sin and all its miserable entailments into human existence, but our neglect to exercise leadership in our homes, church, at work, in our communities has certainly had devastating effects.

But the answer to passivity is not mere activity, but a Spirit-empowered, gospel-grounded, grace-saturated pursuit of courageous intentionality. The burden to lead, protect, and provide is great, but God has provided everything we need in Christ, in His Word, in His Church, and in His Spirit. Once we begin to walk in faith-motivated obedience, we will find that God's commandments are not burdensome (1 John 5:3).

We will also find that it is deeply satisfying to walk in mature manhood. We are men. This may sound obvious, but in our day of rampant gender confusion, it must be affirmed: our manhood is central to who we are as humans. We think, feel, perceive, work, love, pray, worship, and grow spiritually *as men*. Discipleship for us is growing in greater maturity *as men*. And it will always be so. God is glorified, not in humankind generically, but in the particularities of man and woman, each fulfilling their callings according to their respective gender.

When we resist our calling as men, we are conspiring to hide the particular glories of God behind a riddled fence of ambiguity. But we are also working against our joy, for we will find the most satisfaction as we walk, by grace, according to God's design. If our masculinity is central to our very personhood, it is no wonder that we wander in confusion and depression when we neglect to walk in godly masculinity. When we trade leadership for passivity, courage for cowardice, and hard work for laziness, we may find brief, short-term pleasure, but it will never compare to the deep, enduring joys of following after Christ on the path of godly masculinity.

It is my prayer, therefore, that the words in this book—insofar as they align with and help illumine the truth of God's Word—help you to take strides in your pursuit of godly manhood. God is good, and He is wise. His calling for men is glorious, challenging, and deeply satisfying. So, in light of God's mercy in the gospel and by the power of the Holy Spirit, I exhort you, with Paul, to "act like men," for the glory of God, the good of others, and your lasting happiness.

Appendix

Admonish the Idle:
Thoughts on How to Motivate Lazy Men[1]

As we sat down to lunch, it became apparent that this brother whom I had recently met was depressed, full of anxiety, and generally discouraged about his circumstances. He didn't have a plan for life after college, nor did he have a job. He was now in graduate school, but he wasn't sure why. He was still living off his parents and most of his time was spent in his dorm room doing who knows what.

It is difficult to see a man who is given over to listlessness and laziness; something in us recognizes that his unwillingness to work, plan, and forge ahead in life is contrary to God's design. Most would agree: the sluggard's sleepy-eyed approach to life is discouraging to those who have opportunity to observe it. By contrast, men who have a zest for life and a zeal to make significant contributions to their family, church, and society not only possess a genuine attractiveness, but they also motivate people around them to make the most of their own time on earth.

I admit there have been seasons of sloth in my own life. Many times I have neglected important responsibilities to watch television, or surfed the Internet while resisting schoolwork, or even procrastinated in the face of difficult projects. Yet, I must also confess that, when I succumb to the lull of passivity and indolence, I am afterward never satisfied. The sweet promise of pleasure that laziness offers always turns to gravel in my mouth.

Why Should We Seek to Motivate Lazy Men?

When it comes to our labor in the church and among Christian brothers, we should desire their unwavering pursuit of diligence for at least three reasons. First, a pattern of diligence and a strong work ethic fulfills a significant part of their calling as Christian men. Man was created in the image of God and recreated in the image of Christ to work, and work a lot (Gen 1:26-31; 2:15). A man's unwillingness to work is a rebellion against the Lord and a rebellion against a fundamental facet of his personhood.

Second, a solid example of masculine industriousness provides encouragement to other brothers to set their hand to the plow and do something with their lives (2 Thess 3:7-8; Heb 13:7). I am daily motivated to pursue godly productivity by other men in our church, by my pastors, and by my heroes in the faith. Their model of single-minded persistence and productivity is inspiring, to say the least.

Finally, we should lovingly admonish our brothers because we are convinced that the path of obedience is the path of true satisfaction. We know and they know (if they have truly tasted it) that only a life of Spirit-empowered labor for the glory of God is truly fulfilling—if only they could get off the couch. The rest of this article aims to help them do just that.

Nine Ways to Motivate Lazy Men

Give Them a Compelling Vision of What They Could Be

It may be tempting to approach a lazy brother with the exclusive use of exhortation: "Get up! Do something! Be a man!" There is a place for this kind of appeal; the sluggard will typically need patient yet prodding words to wake him from his slumber. I will talk more about this form of motivation below, but at this point it is vital to remember our speech must involve more than in-your-face locker room talk. Men need a compelling vision of what they could be.

Scripture does not merely give us negative admonitions and rebukes; nearly every time Solomon offers a cautionary description of the lazy, foolish man, he precedes or follows such warnings with counter examples of the diligent, wise man. Our pattern should be similar.

Rather than only telling our lethargic friend he will suffer loss if he follows his current path, we should also make the effort to place before him a picture of what he could be if he would turn from his folly and pursue a life of gospel-motivated diligence. Jesus Christ is in the business of taking wandering, listless, lethargic boys and transforming them into decisive, purposeful, active men. So help your brother see that he could be, by God's grace, a Christ-like husband, a courageous father, a productive employee, a fruitful church member, a respected neighbor, and an influential leader. You will be amazed at how a positive vision of godly masculinity will motivate a man to find his way out of an idle existence.[2]

Remove Their Objections

As we deliver this vision of what our brother could be, we must be ready to dismantle his objections. If he knows the

Lord Jesus, he possesses the spiritual resources necessary for a life of gospel fruitfulness. He must grasp this essential truth if he is going to make headway out of the mire of his purposelessness.

Now, I don't mean to suggest that one's past, personality, or present circumstances are irrelevant— we must exercise compassion with our brothers in Christ and seek to really understand why they are having so much trouble getting out of bed in the morning. But in order to combat the discouragement that assuredly pervades their life, we must bring men to a place where they are convinced there are no permanent barriers between where they are now and where God would have them be in the future. They can find forgiveness in Christ for their past sins. God is gracious and merciful, slow to anger, and abounding in steadfast love (Ex 34:6–7). Their Savior has given to all Christians everything pertaining to life and godliness (2 Pet 1:3–4).

By removing your brother's objections you are not being unkind; you are giving him hope that halts the way laziness feeds discouragement, and vice versa. Eliminate all objections, and you have done much to stop his vicious cycle of apathy and despair.

Help Them Understand Work is
Essential to Being Human
Although they may claim to know what Scripture teaches on the issue of vocation, you cannot take the depth of their knowledge for granted. They must see afresh how pervasive the theme of work is in Scripture, and how sloth is a sinful rejection of a fundamental component of their humanity. To be made in the image of God means, first and foremost, that we are to exercise dominion over the earth for the sake of

human flourishing (Gen 1:26–31). Man was designed for the purpose of work (Gen 2:15). Thus, the refusal to work is a sure sign of foolishness (Prov 12:11) that impoverishes a person physically and spiritually (Prov 6:9–11; 10:4). Indeed, the one who is lazy is closely related to one who destroys (Prov 18:9) and is in need of a stern rebuke (2 Thess 3:6–11; Titus 1:13).

If it is true, then, that work is fundamental to human personhood, refusal to work will naturally lead to problems in other areas of life. Thus, you must make a direct connection between a person's anxiety, depression, and lack of fulfillment with their refusal to work. Help your brother consider that their spiritual condition may in large part be due to their unwillingness to do what God created them to do. While it may be difficult to determine whether one's laziness caused the depression or the reverse, we must acknowledge that to remain in a state of perpetual lethargy will most assuredly lead to more depression.[3]

Show Them From Scripture What
Happens to a Lazy Person
Not only must we offer positive encouragement, we must also help our brothers see what their future holds if they continue in their current path: spiritual and physical poverty (Prov 10:4–5; 12:11; 19:15), unshakable feelings of purposelessness (Prov 15:19), despondency, depression, and a life devoid of real accomplishment awaits them (Prov 10:26; 13:4; 20:4; 21:25–26).[4] Find a way to help your brother taste the bitterness of these fruits before they are in full harvest in his own life. In the same way you painted a picture of wonderful possibilities, cast for them a vision of dreadful

consequences, praying that the Spirit might make their sloth morally reprehensible and utterly unattractive.

Explain to Them How the Curse Has Affected Their Manhood

While we seek to show our brothers that work is essential to their humanity and that laziness leads only to loss, it will also be necessary to help them see that the path of diligence will often be the path of most resistance. The conflict they experience is a direct result of the fall of humankind into sin. Explain to them that after the fall, God cursed an aspect of creation that is central to their masculine calling (see Gen 3:17–19). Temptation to passivity and laziness is now compounded by the fact that work is difficult, occasionally fruitless, and will not often yield satisfaction until a man has expended significant effort. A right understanding of the curse is essential for helping men cultivate a life of diligence, for they must know that they are fighting an uphill battle lest they become discouraged.

Ask Them About Pornography

In his first epistle, Peter exhorts his readers to abstain from fleshly lusts because they "wage war against the soul" (1 Pet 2:11). Peter's use of the word "soul" (Gr. *psyche*) in his admonishment is instructive, because it tells us that the apostle intends to ground our motivation for abstinence from lust in the well-being of our *whole* inner-person. An addiction to pornography doesn't merely wreak havoc on the mind; it devastates the affections and the will. Lust robs men of ambition, discourages initiative, perverts inclinations, sabotages desire for godly productivity, promotes passivity, dampens passion for adventure, hinders taste for spiritual truth, and weakens the ability to concentrate. It could be that the brother you are seeking to encourage in a path of diligence is caught in a slough of lust. Ask him about pornography.[5]

Address the Assurance of their Salvation

We cannot confine our admonishments to only address temporal troubles. Scripture indicates there are eternal issues to be considered in relation to one's tendency toward sloth. In Jesus' parable of the talents, for example, we learn that an unproductive life is evidence that one may not know the Lord. The man who hid his one talent because he perceived his master as a hard, unfair man received a damning rebuke for his laziness and a promise of eternal punishment (Matt 25:24–26).

We must communicate straightforwardly to our lazy brother that he should not expect an abiding sense of assurance of his salvation so long as he remains in his current condition. While salvation does not come by our works of obedience, assurance of our salvation certainly does. A professing Christian who resides in a perpetual state of idleness cannot have assurance that the energizing, fruit-producing, work-compelling Spirit resides in him.[6]

Be Firm

While it is vital that we warm our brother's affections by providing a compelling vision of what is possible in his life, it is equally essential that we apply an appropriate amount of forthright admonishment to wake him from his slumber. Paul says, "admonish the idle" (1 Thess 5:14). The book of Proverbs makes it clear that rebuke is the way of wisdom. Irresolute, timid, inconsequential suggestions rarely—if ever—make their way deep into the heart of the lazy man. He is right in his own eyes (Prov 26:16) and therefore desperately needs strong, straightforward, unflinching, eye-to-eye rebuke for wasting the life God has given him. Be firm.

Be Patient

In the same verse where Paul instructs the Thessalonians to admonish the idle, he reminds us to be patient. The apostle recognized a tendency in all of us to grow exasperated with our brothers and throw up our hands in resignation as their progress sputters and stalls. Our frustration, however, will only prove deadly to their growth and is probably rooted in our own self-righteousness. It is likely that change will be gradual, so we must resolve to make consistent effort to persevere through seemingly fruitless seasons. "Let us not grow weary of doing good," the apostle reminds us, "for in due season we will reap, if we do not give up" (Gal 6:9). Be patient.

Final Thoughts

Even though I have offered several strategies to spur on a lazy brother to love and good deeds, I do not mean to imply that such a list is exhaustive. The labor required to understand your friend and pinpoint the root cause of his troubles is complicated and demanding. Below the surface of an indolent life lurk deeper issues of the heart, and only a man of understanding is able to draw them out (Prov 20:5). So, I have not attempted to address all the issues related to the topic of laziness; rather, I have offered a few basic principles to help guide you in your efforts to counsel your brother to get off the couch and fulfill the calling God has for him.

NOTES

Introduction

1. Gary Cross, *Men to Boys: The Making of Modern Immaturity* (New York: Columbia University Press, 2008), 1.

Chapter One – One Man's Passivity

1. We can say that there is no ontological superiority of the man over the woman. That is, both the man and woman are fully God's image (see Gen 1:27). Their "being"—what makes them human—is the same, although their roles as men and women will differ. For an excellent discussion of the differences between man and woman understood within the context of their equality, see Raymond C. Ortland, Jr., "Male and Female Equality and Male Headship: Genesis 1-3," in *Recovering Biblical Manhood and Womanhood: A Response to Evangelical Feminism*, eds. John Piper and Wayne Grudem (Wheaton, IL: Crossway, 2006), 95-112.

2. For more on the Christian doctrine of work, see Richard Steele, *The Religious Tradesman* (1747; Harrisonburg, VA: Sprinkle Publications, 1989); Timothy Keller, *Every Good Endeavor: Connecting Your Work with God's Work* (New York: Dutton, 2012); Chad Brand, *Flourishing Faith: A Baptist Primer on Work, Economics, and Civic Stewardship* (Grand Rapids: Christian's Library Press, 2012); Gene Veith, *God at Work: Your Christian Vocation in All of Life* (Wheaton: Crossway, 2002); and Sabastian Trager and Greg Gilbert *The Gospel at Work: How Working for King Jesus Gives Purpose and Meaning to Our Jobs* (Grand Rapids: Zondervan, 2013). See also my essay, "Admonish the Idle: Thoughts for How to Motivate Lazy Men," in the appendix of this book for more on the vital connection between manhood and work.

3. Sinclair Ferguson, *The Whole Christ: Legalism, Antinomianism, and Gospel Assurance—Why the Marrow Controversy Still Matters* (Wheaton: Crossway, 2016), 80.

4. At this point I must note that I take the first and second chapters of Genesis as complementary descriptions of one creation account, not two different creation stories. It has been argued by some biblical scholars that the author of Genesis presents us with distinct creation stories that cannot be reconciled with respect to the chronology of the man and woman's creation, and should, therefore, be read symbolically. The text of Genesis, however, does not require that we propose two different creation accounts. Instead, a better and more natural solution is to see Moses providing us in Genesis 1:26-31 with a broad description of man's creation on day six, to then turn in Genesis 2:1ff to give a detailed description of what occurred on that day. In Genesis 1:26-31, we are told that God created both the man and the woman on the sixth day. Genesis 2:1ff tells us that Adam and Eve came into existence in a particular order: the man first, then the woman. See Derek Kidner, *Genesis: Introduction and Commentary* (Downers Grove, IL: Intervarsity, 1967), 58; C. John Collins, *Genesis 1-4: A Linguistic, Literary, and Theological Commentary* (Philipsburg, NJ: P & R, 2006), 108-112.

5. Scripture seems to indicate that God created the angels before He created the earth. Note Job 38:4-7 where God asks Job, "Where were you when I laid the foundation of the earth? Tell me, if you have understanding. Who determined its measurements—surely you know! Or who stretched the line upon it? On what were its bases sunk, or who laid its cornerstone, when the morning stars sang together and all the sons of God shouted for joy?" Several commentators take "sons of God" to refer to angels. If this is the case, then regardless of the timing of Satan's fall, then it is true that he would have observed the entire process of the man and woman's creation.

6. It might be argued that we can't be dogmatic about whether or not Adam was with Eve during Satan's initial conversation with her. Although I agree there is room to be flexible at this point and suggest that Adam could have been elsewhere during Satan's conversation with Eve, I believe four pieces of evidence in this

text lead us to conclude that Adam was with his wife during the entire encounter with Satan.

First, we have already learned in Genesis 2:18 that it was not good for man to be alone. In response to this situation, God created a woman in order to remedy this lack in Adam's life. Having created the perfect complement to the man, the man and woman were to become "one flesh" in sexual union. Indeed, the end of chapter two reports that the man and the woman were both "naked and unashamed" (Gen 2:25). When we come to chapter three, it is reasonable to assume that Adam and Eve would have been together given the fact that she was created for the very purpose of companionship and that they already had or were about ready to become one flesh. In other words, its natural to expect that Adam and Eve are together as we come to the events in chapter three.

Second, when Satan addresses Eve, he inquires about the commandment God had given regarding from what trees the man and the woman could eat. "Did God actually say," Satan asks, "'You shall not eat of any tree in the garden'" (Gen 3:1)? Although one cannot see this in the English translation, the Hebrew indicates that when God gave this original commandment to Adam, He addressed the man in the singular: "...but of the tree of the knowledge of good and evil, *you* shall not eat" (Gen 2:17, emphasis added). When Satan asks Eve about this commandment, he uses the plural. "Did God actually say, '*You* shall not eat of any tree in the garden" (emphasis added). Eve then replies in the plural: "*We* may eat of the fruit of the trees of the garden, neither shall *you* touch it, lest *you* die." Satan responds again in the plural: "*You* will not surely die! For God knows that when *you* eat of it *your* eyes will be opened, and *you* will be like God, knowing good and evil" (Gen 3:4-5, emphasis added). The fact that Eve and the serpent discuss God's commandment by using plural pronouns seems to imply that the man was with her during this time.

Third, when Eve takes of the fruit and gives it to her husband, the text says that he was "with her." The question we need to ask is why Moses included this bit of information? To say that the woman gave the fruit to her husband implies that he was with her, for how else would she give him the fruit? In other words, the phrase "with her" is simply redundant unless Moses means to indicate that the man was with her during the entire episode, not just at the giving of the fruit.

Fourth, immediately after Adam eats of the fruit, the man and the woman's eyes were opened. The first thing they notice is their nakedness. The last place nakedness was mentioned was in Gen 2:25 where the text says that the couple were both "naked and unashamed." By situating the account of the serpent's deception between these to references to nakedness, it seems that Moses is indicating that what was true in the first reference to nakedness was true until the second mention of nakedness; namely, that the man and woman were together.

None of these four pieces of evidence taken individually prove that Adam was with Eve during the entire temptation from Satan's initial approach to Eve's eating of the fruit. But together they build a cumulative case that strongly suggests that Adam was with his wife the whole time.

7. Recently, after teaching on this passage, I was asked by two thoughtful graduate students when Eve actually disobeyed. Did she sin in doubting God's goodness, or was the sin in the actual eating? Although this question might appear to engage in some unwarranted speculation, the answer, I believe, actually lies squarely in the text. God had specifically warned Adam and Eve that they were to not eat of the fruit of the tree or they would surely die (Gen 2:17). Therefore, I take the actual sin to have occurred at the moment of eating. The doubting of God's goodness, which was probably one of the underlying motives for Eve's taking of the fruit, was not brought to sinful consummation until she at the fruit. It was at the very moment that Eve at the fruit that she *finally disbelieved* God's Word. Prior to the actual eating of the fruit, Eve would have only been wrestling with the temptation to doubt God's goodness. But at the eating of the fruit, Eve fully embraced the lie and doubted God. But the sin of unbelief and the actual sin of eating are so closely connected that it is impossible to separate.

8. We have to make clear at this point that Adam's sin was in the eating of the fruit, not in his actions leading up to his eating the fruit. God's original command warned only against eating of the

fruit of the tree of the knowledge of good and evil (see Gen 2:17). Paul calls this Adam's "one act of disobedience" (Rom 5:19) in which Adam sinned willfully, not as a result of deception (see 1 Tim 2:14). We also know that it was at the point of eating the fruit that Adam sinned because it was immediately after eating that "the eyes of both were opened" (Gen 3:7). Nevertheless, when God applies the curse to Adam, He tells the man that he would endure the curse precisely because he (1) listened to the voice of his wife; and (2) ate of the forbidden fruit (see Gen 3:17). We might argue, then, that passivity was so intertwined with Adam's act of disobedience that we can't ultimately separate it from the actual transgression, although we can distinguish the two. We might say that Adam's passivity wasn't the transgression *per se*, but it inevitably led to the transgression. This point is similar to what I said about Eve's sin in the previous footnote. The question there was when did Eve's sin occur? Was it in her doubting of God's goodness or in the actual eating of the fruit? The text only allows us to say that she sinned at the eating of the fruit. It was at the very point of eating, therefore, that she finally disbelieved God's Word. In Adam's case, he finally yielded to passivity at the point of actively eating the fruit.

9. Douglas Wilson, *Reforming Marriage* (Moscow, ID: Canon Press, 1995), 24.

Chapter Two – The Character of Mature Manhood

1. What I have in mind here are the traditional ways, at least in Western culture, that men have honored women. Some examples would be a men holding doors open for women, men standing up at the table when a woman enters or leaves the room, men defending women from violent perpetrators, and so on.

2. See John Piper, "A Vision of Biblical Complementarity," in *Recovering Biblical Manhood and Womanhood,* eds. John Piper and Wayne Grudem (Wheaton, IL: Crossway, 2006): 39.

3. John Stott, *The Letters of John,* Tyndale New Testament Commentaries (Grand Rapids, Eerdmans, 1988), 99.

4. John Calvin, *The Institutes of the Christian Religion*, ed. John T. Maxwell, trans. Ford Lewis Battles, vol. 2 (Philadelphia: Westminster Press, 1960), 1509.

5. J. Oswald Sanders, *Dynamic Spiritual Leadership: Leading Like Paul* (Grand Rapids: Discovery House Publishers, 1999), 51.

6. Sanders, *Dynamic Spiritual Leadership*, 51.

7. Jay Adams, *Teaching to Observe: The Counselor as Teacher* (Woodruff, SC: Timeless Texts, 1995), 124.

Chapter Three – The Calling of Mature Manhood: Leadership

1. I am indebted to John Piper's work in his article, "A Vision of Biblical Complementarity: Manhood and Womanhood Defined According to the Bible" for helping me craft this definition of mature masculinity. See *Recovering Biblical Manhood and Womanhood: A Response to Evangelical Feminism* (Wheaton, IL: Crossway, 2006), 31-59.

2. In the past and even today some Christian teachers argue that it is possible to achieve a kind of perfection in this life where willful (as opposed to inadvertent) sin is no longer a problem for the mature believer. This teaching is not only contrary to Scripture; it can cause significant problems for the Christian, including intense discouragement and depression, spiritual pride, and self-deception. The Scriptures tell us that although Christians have a new nature, they will fight and struggle with sin—even a temptation to commit willful sin—until they reach heaven (see Rom 7:14-23; Col 3:1-7).

3. John MacArthur, *The Book on Leadership* (Nashville: Thomas Nelson, 2004), 37.

4. For a concise yet very helpful discussion of discerning God's will, I recommend Kevin DeYoung's, *Just Do Something: A Liberating Approach to Finding God's Will* (Chicago: Moody, 2014).

5. David McCullough, *1776* (New York: Simon and Schuster, 2005), 161.

Chapter Four – The Calling of Mature Manhood: Protection

1. John Piper, "A Vision of Biblical Complementarity," in *Recovering Biblical Manhood and Womanhood*, ed. John Piper and Wayne Grudem (Wheaton, IL: Crossway, 2006), 43-44.

2. For help in this area, especially with regard to church settings, see Deepak Reju's *On Guard: Preventing and Responding to Child Abuse at Church* (Greensboro, NC: New Growth Press, 2014).

3. Steven J. Lawson, *The Legacy: What Every Father Wants to Leave His Child* (Colorado Springs: Multnomah, 1998), 182.
4. See for example, Dr. Nicholas Kardaras, "'It's Digital Heroin': How Screens are Turning Kids into Psychotic Junkies," *NY Post*, August 27, 2016. Accessed September 28, 2016, http://nypost.com/2016/08/27/its-digital-heroin-how-screens-turn-kids-into-psychotic-junkies.
5. See Tony Reinke, "Smart Phone Addiction and Our Spiritual ADD," *DesiringGod.org*, April 18, 2015. Accessed December 30, 2015, http://www.desiringgod.org/articles/smartphone-addiction-and-our-spiritual-add.
6. Dave Harvey, *When Sinners Say 'I Do': Discovering the Power of the Gospel for Marriage* (Wapwallopen, PA, 2007), 163.
7. For encouragement in this area of pursuing and romancing your wife, I recommend C. J. Mahaney's little book, *Sex, Romance, and the Glory of God* (Wheaton, IL: Crossway, 2004), and Stuart Scott's chapter, "A Husband's Responsibility – Physical Intimacy," in his book, *The Exemplary Husband: A Biblical Perspective*, Revised Edition (Bemidji, MN: Focus, 2002), 143-155.
8. For more on how to understand this passage and how saving faith is lust-fighting faith, see John Piper, *The Purifying Power of Living By Faith in Future Grace* (Sisters, OR: Multnomah, 1995), 329-338.
9. The phrase "the Spirit and the gifts are yours" is taken from one of my favorite hymns, written by Martin Luther, "A Mighty Fortress is our God" (1529).

Chapter Five – The Calling of Mature Manhood: Provision

1. For example, see Jaye Martin and Terri Stovall, *Women Leading Women: The Biblical Model for the Church* (Nashville: B&H Academic, 2008); Elizabeth Elliot, *Let Me Be a Woman* (Wheaton, IL: Tyndale House, 1999); Carolyn Mahaney, *Feminine Appeal: Seven Virtues of a Godly Wife and Mother* (Wheaton: Crossway, 2004); Courtney Reissig, *The Accidental Feminist: Restoring our Delight in God's Good Design*; Dorothy Patterson, "The High Calling of Wife and Mother in Biblical Perspective," in *Recovering Biblical Manhood and Womanhood*, 364-77; Dee Jepson, "Women in Society: The Challenge and the Call," in *Recovering Biblical Manhood and Womanhood*, 388-93; and Elizabeth Elliot, "The Essence of

Femininity: A Personal Perspective," in *Recovering Biblical Manhood and Womanhood*, 394-99.

2. Russell Moore, *Adopted for Life: The Priority of Adoption for Christian Families and Churches* (Wheaton, IL: Crossway, 2009), 70.

3. Of course, not all women will be married, and not all women who are married will be able to bear children. In these cases, it might be more challenging for a woman to avoid temptations to idleness. Given Paul's commendation of singleness, however, we can have confidence that women without a husband and children can live a life of fruitful service to God (see 1 Cor 7:8; 34-35). But the reality that some women may never marry or have children does not change the fact that Paul recognizes a fundamental difference between men and women's roles. Generally speaking, the man is expected to be the provider, and the woman is expected to care for the home and children.

4. Frederick William Danker, ed., *A Greek-English Lexicon of the New Testament and Other Early Christian Literature*, 3rd edition (Chicago: The University of Chicago Press, 2000), 311.

5. John Piper, *This Momentary Marriage*, 86-87.

6. See Gretchen Livingston, "Growing Number of Dads at Home with Kids," *The Pew Research Center*, June 5, 2014. Accessed February 24, 2017. http://www.pewsocialtrends.org/2014/06/05/growing-number-of-dads-home-with-the-kids/.

Chapter Six – On Leaving Father and Mother

1. See Richard Fry, "For the First Time in Modern Era, Living with Parents Edges out Other Living Arrangements for 18-34 Year Olds," *The Pew Research Center*, May 24, 2016. accessed February 24, 2017, http://www.pewsocialtrends.org/2016/05/24/for-first-time-in-modern-era-living-with-parents-edges-out-other-living-arrangements-for-18-to-34-year-olds/.

2. Mark 3:20-21 only mentions "his family." The text reads, "Then he went home, and the crowd gathered again, so that they could not even eat. And when his family heard it, they went out to seize him, for they were saying, 'He is out of his mind.'" A few verses later, Mark mentions Jesus' "mother and his brothers" who had come to find Jesus while He was preaching (see Mark 3:31-35). It could be, then, that by leaving out the reference to Jesus' mother

in 3:21, Mark means to indicate that only His brothers and other relatives were the ones who thought Jesus was "out of his mind." Or, Mark could just as likely meant to include Jesus' mother among those who thought Jesus was out of His mind, and the word "family" is merely shorthand for "mother and brothers." The context does not allow us to be dogmatic either way. Luke 2:41-51 and John 2:4, however, both lend to the notion that Mary didn't fully comprehend Jesus' ministry in its initial stages.

Chapter Seven – Singleness and Mature Manhood

1. For a helpful discussion of singleness from a whole-bible perspective, I recommend Barry Danylak, *Redeeming Singleness: How the Storyline of Scripture Affirms the Single Life* (Wheaton, IL: Crossway, 2010).

2. R. V. G. Tasker, quoted in J. I. Packer, *Knowing God* (Downer's Grove, IL: IVP, 1993), 170.

3. This phrase is found in traditional wedding vows. "Do you promise to love her, comfort her, honor and keep her for better or worse, for richer or poorer, in sickness and health, and forsaking all others, be faithful only to her, for as long as you both shall live?"

4. Jay Adams, *Christian Living in the Home* (Philipsburg, NJ: P & R, 1972), 64.

5. Adams, *Christian Living in the Home*, 64.

6. Adams, *Christian Living in the Home*, 64.

7. Stuart Scott, *The Exemplary Husband: A Biblical Perspective*, Revised Version (Bemidji, MN: Focus, 2002), 242.

8. These points were brought out by John Piper in an "Ask Pastor John" podcast at DesiringGod.org. See "Could a Complementarian/Egalitarian Marriage Work?" May 26, 2106. Accessed February 3, 2017,df http://www.desiringgod.org/interviews/could-a-complementarian-egalitarian-marriage-work.

9. Moore, *Adopted for Life*, 72.

10. I first heard this catchy proverb from Jeff Elieff, my former pastor at 9th and O Baptist Church in Louisville, Kentucky.

11. This is a phrase I first heard from John Piper. David Mathis, executive producer at Desiring God Ministries, explains what Piper means by the phrase. "It's a vision for the Christian to

steer a middle course between idolizing our bodies and neglecting them. It includes giving our bodies enough attention — with sleep, diet, exercise, and upkeep — to avoid being distractingly unattractive, and reining in our impulses to pursue a self-focused attractiveness that distracts." David Mathis, "Dieting, Botox, and Honoring God with Your Body," DesiringGod.org, October 2, 2013. Accessed February 24, 2017, http://www.desiringgod.org/articles/dieting-botox-and-honoring-jesus-with-your-body.

12. *Pornography Statistics: 250+ Facts, Quotes, and Statistics About Porn Use*, 2015 edition (Owosso, MI: Covenant Eyes, 2015), 8.

Chapter Eight – The Resources You Need (and Have in Christ!)

1. "Fifth Severed Foot Found on Canadian Coast," June 17, 2008. Accessed December 2, 2016, http://www.cnn.com/2008/CRIME/06/17/canada.feet/

2. For an excellent and accessible introduction to the history and theology of the Reformation, I highly recommend Michael Reeves and Tim Chester, *Why the Reformation Still Matters* (Wheaton, IL: Crossway, 2016).

3. Gary Cross, *Men to Boys: The Making of Modern Immaturity* (New York: Columbia University Press, 2008), 18.

Appendix – Admonish the Idle: Thoughts for How to Motivate Lazy Men

1. This appendix is adapted from my article that originally appeared in *The Journal of Biblical Manhood and Womanhood* 20.1 (Spring 2015), 19-23. Used by Permission.

2. A couple of recent books for providing you many useful ideas for helping men see what they could be are Matt Perman, *What's Best Next: How the Gospel Transforms the Way You Get things Done* (Grand Rapids: Zondervan, 2014) and Dave Harvey, *Rescuing Ambition* (Wheaton, IL: Crossway, 2010).

3. I recognize that uncovering the root causes of one's depression can be a complex and difficult process. Nevertheless, I believe it is unwise to allow a person who is struggling with depression to remain in a perpetual state of sloth, for they cannot expect much deliverance from their depression so long as they are refusing to

work. Applying oneself to one's responsibilities can often serve as the first step out of depression. See Jay E. Adams, *Competent to Counsel: Introduction to Nouthetic Counseling* (Grand Rapids: Zondervan, 1970), 143-44.

4. Bruce Waltke insightfully observes that Proverbs 13:4 ("The soul of the sluggard craves and gets nothing, while the soul of the diligent is richly supplied" [ESV]) includes all human appetites in its chastisement of the lazy man: the sluggard is unable to acquire or accomplish *anything* of significance! "By contrast, the sluggard's appetite is not fattened but *craves. . . and he has not...*The unqualified *wa'ayin* refers to everything his human drives and appetites aspire to, such as eating (Job 33:20; Mic 7:1), drinking (2 Sam 23:15), and the opposite sex (Ps 45:11[12]; Jer. 2:24). The antithesis implies that every appetite of the diligent person is abundantly satisfied, including his hunger for God (see Pss 42:1[2]; 63:1[2]). The proverb assumes that everything needful in life is richly available under God's good hand (Ps 128:1–3), but it is non-existent for the sluggard (Ps 128:1)." Bruce K. Waltke, *The Book of Proverbs: Chapters 1–15*, The New International Commentary on the Old Testament; (Grand Rapids: Eerdmans, 2004), 554–55.

5. For some excellent help in the area of sexual purity and finding victory over pornography addiction, see Heath Lambert *Finally Free: Fighting for Purity by the Power of Grace* (Grand Rapids: Zondervan, 2013) and Tim Challies, *Sexual Detox: A Guide for Guys Who Are Sick of Porn* (Adelphi, MD: Cruciform Press, 2010).

6. While you will not be able to say definitively that the professing brother in this case is an unbeliever due to his laziness (for only God can see the heart), you can safely question his assurance of salvation based on his unwillingness to diligently steward the Lord's resources. For an excellent discussion of perseverance, assurance, and the role of warnings in Scripture, see Thomas R. Schreiner, "Perseverance and Assurance: A Survey and a Proposal" *SBJT* 2.1 (Spring 1998), 32– 62. Schreiner has also expanded on these ideas in a book co-authored with Ardel B. Caneday. See Thomas R. Schreiner and Ardel B. Caneday, *The Race Set Before Us: A Biblical Theology of Perseverance and Assurance* (Downers Grove, IL: IVP Academic, 2001).

Scripture Index

About the Author

Originally from Montana, Derek received his undergraduate degree from The Master's College (Santa Clarita, CA) and his M.Div. and Ph.D. from Southern Baptist Theological Seminary (Louisville, KY). He previously served as the managing editor of *The Journal of Discipleship and Family Ministry*, and as adjunct professor of Christian Theology at the Southern Baptist Theological Seminary. He is the author of *How to Pray for Your Pastor* (GBF Press) and currently serves as an associate pastor at Grace Bible Fellowship of Silicon Valley where he oversees the college and young adult ministry. Derek lives with his wife and two boys in the San Francisco Bay Area. You can find him online at FromTheStudy.com.

.